Lukács and Heidegger

Lukács and Heidegger

Towards a new philosophy

Lucien Goldmann

Translated by William Q. Boelhower

Routledge & Kegan Paul
London, Henley and Boston

This translation first published in 1977
by Routledge & Kegan Paul Ltd
39 Store Street
London WC1E 7DD,
Broadway House
Newtown Road
Henley-on-Thames
Oxon RG9 1EN and
9 Park Street
Boston, Mass. 02108, USA
First published as a paperback 1979
Set in IBM Journal Roman by
Express Litho Service, Oxford
and printed in Great Britain by
Unwin Brothers Limited
The Gresham Press, Old Woking, Surrey
A member of the Staples Printing Group
Translated from Lukács et Heidegger
French edition © Editions Denoël 1973
Part III © Presses Universitaires de France 1960
English Translation © Routledge & Kegan Paul 1977

British Library Cataloguing in Publication Data

Goldman, Lucien
Lukács and Heidegger.
1. Lukács, György   2. Heidegger, Martin
I. Title II. Boelhower, William Q
199'.439   B4815.L84   77—30136

ISBN 0—7100—8625—3
ISBN 0—7100—8794—2 Pbk

Contents

Publisher's Note   vii

A Glossary of the Important Terms and
Concepts in *Lukács and Heidegger*   ix

Part 1
Introduction to Lukács and Heidegger   1

Part 2
Lectures during the 1967—8 Academic Year   25

1   Reification, *Zuhandenheit* and Praxis   27

2   Totality, Being and History   40

3   Objective Possibility and Possible
Consciousness   52

4   Subject-object and Function   67

5   The Topicality of the Question of the Subject   86

Part 3
Being and Dialectics   99

Notes   110

Publisher's Note

In this edition of *Lukács and Heidegger* the translator has included a glossary of words which Lucien Goldmann uses in special ways in this book.

We have included an article by Lucien Goldmann, 'Being and Dialectics' which was published in *Études Philosophiques* in 1960, which seems particularly relevant to the ideas in the book, and have omitted M. Ishaghpour's preface to the French edition, which seems relevant principally to French readers, and not to the Anglophone world.

Although he had already begun to study the philosophical relations between the early writings of Lukács and Heidegger as early as 1945, Lucien Goldmann only finished writing Part I (Introduction to Lukács and Heidegger) of his projected book begun in August 1970. Part II of *Lukács and Heidegger*, instead, is composed of transcripts from tapes of his lectures given during the winter of 1967–8 at the École pratique des Hautes Études. As a result, these chapters are more loosely organized and occasionally repetitious.

RKP

A Glossary of the Important Terms and Concepts in *Lukács and Heidegger*

Since *Lukács and Heidegger* is a confluence of three different philosophical positions (there is as much Goldmann here as there is Heidegger and Lukács), and since the book is based on lectures given to university students already acquainted with the philosophies under discussion, this *selected* glossary may help the uninitiated reader who, even if he has read the Lukács and Heidegger texts, probably has not read Goldmann, for the greater part of the latter's thought has still not been translated into English. A word of caution, however. In no instance can the glosses be considered as substitutes for the lengthy treatment these terms are given in *Being and Time* and *History and Class Consciousness*. They are merely meant as immediate clarifications, since Goldmann's own position, which is not presented systematically here, contextualizes these concepts in a particular way. I have added the German and French words, respectively, when I thought it would help solve possible confusions created by the translation. The quotations are taken from the published English translations of Heidegger's *Being and Time* (New York: Harper & Row, 1962) and Lukács's *History and Class Consciousness* (Cambridge, Mass.: MIT Press, 1972). I would, finally, like to acknowledge and thank the publishers of those two books for permission to use their editions.

William Q. Boelhower

AUTHENTIC/eigentlich/authentique

Heidegger describes the possibilities of Being-there (*Dasein*) as being either authentic or inauthentic. These two possibilities are permanently and abstractly before the individual who must choose between these two modes of living. An authentic life is one lived in the consciousness of limit and of being-free-for-death through a resolute-decision. Being-there grasps its Being when it lives authentically. A synonym which Heidegger uses for this term is 'real'.

Cf. Being-there, inauthentic, resolute-decision.

BEING/Sein/Être

The question of the meaning of Being, which has an ontological priority over ontical questions, is posed in strict connection with the meaning of Being-there. From this latter, Being is described as historical and temporal. Only phenomenological ontology is methodologically capable of asking the question of the meaning of Being, according to Heidegger. Lukács's category, which operates in a similar fashion, is 'totality'.

Cf. ontic, ontology, totality.

BEING-THERE/Dasein/Être-là

This is Heidegger's term for the individual, who only exists in so far as a being-in-the-world, in the condition of thrownness.

BEING-TOWARD-DEATH/Sein zum Tode/Être-pour-la-mort

This is a term describing Being-there's finitude and temporality as its ontological constitution. Death is the central event of Being-there and should be faced consciously, i.e., authentically. It is Being-there's 'ownmost' and 'non-relational' possibility, according to Heidegger.

BEING-WITH/Mitsein/Être-avec

Heidegger's description of the averageness of Being-there as part of the 'they', when an individual's Being is taken away by 'Others', a condition in which everyone is the Other and no one is himself.

Cf. inauthentic, false consciousness, one.

COMMUNITY/Gemeinschaft/La communauté

Being-there, as Being-in-the-world, exists essentially by Being-with Others. The fate of individuals is determined by their being with one another in the same world and by their resoluteness.

Cf. Being-with, resolute-decision.

COMPREHENSION/La compréhension

For Goldmann there is a twofold process in arriving at a total knowledge of an object: comprehension and explanation. To comprehend an object is to describe its internal structure in an exhaustive way.

Cf. explanation.

CRITICAL CONSCIOUSNESS

The philosopher's absolute viewpoint from 'above' history which allows him to carry his critique of society to an extreme degree of negativity, that is, a refusal to identify his critique of society with any of the existing social forces or those in the process of becoming. Goldmann traces this category of Theodor Adorno's to B. Bauer and M. Stirner, and in doing so, finds a subject/object dualism to be characteristic of all three thinkers, whereby the subject is unrelated to all social praxis or concept of historical totality. The reference point for effecting this radical critique Adorno calls 'truth content'.

Cf. truth content.

DESTINY/Geschick/La destinée

Authentic being-with in the community of a people.

DIALECTIC

The unity of theory and praxis, subject and object, and value judgments and judgments of fact. According to dialectical methodology, in order for an object to be understood, it must be linked to its genesis and the subject responsible for its creation. This involves inserting it in a larger totality wherein its mediations are brought to light.

Cf. epistemological circle.

LA DIFFÉRANCE

This term of J. Derrida's is at the basis of all theory and refers to the given, that which is present as a process or force which produces 'les différences' (the differences). The differences produced then make 'la différance', an absence which remains a movement or process that continues to create further differences. See Derrida's *L'Écriture et la différance*.

LA DIFFÉRENCE

The differences are derived from 'la différance', according to Derrida's system. 'La différence' is the concept of particularity: one thing differs from another, renews it, opposes it, thus diversity and specificity. Goldmann maintains that these two categories parallel Heidegger's 'Vorhandenheit' and 'Zuhandenheit', readiness-to-hand and presence-at-hand, respectively.

Cf. readiness-to-hand, presence-at-hand.

EPISTEMOLOGICAL CIRCLE

This concept Goldmann takes from Jean Piaget who, according to Goldmann, proves in an experimental way the Marxist dialectical method of the subject-object unity. The subject is part of the world and introduces meaning there in a practical way, but the world is part of the subject and constitutes it. This unity eliminates the problem of all dualisms which privilege either the subject or the object, theory or praxis, in such a way as inevitably to set one against the other. Their relationship is circular. For Heidegger, too, the question of Being is that of Being-there: the two are dialectically related.

ERLEBNIS

The term for a deeply lived experience, according to W. Dilthey, whose life philosophy is based upon the criteria of such experiences as the source of knowledge. His philosophy, then, is a version of personalism.

Cf. personalism.

EXISTENTIALISM

A philosophical movement which attempts to explain Being or Totality from the perspective of the individual, with the consequence that the individual's consciousness is privileged and reality subjectivized. Goldmann considers Lukács to be the founder of modern existentialism with his book *The Soul and the Forms*. Heidegger's *Being and Time* is another, but different, example. Both works, however, conceive of man as a being in the world and inseparable from it, with death being the essential event for him.

EXPLANATION/L'explication

To explain an object is to place it within a vaster structure whereby its functionality and genesis are revealed, as well as its significance and essential coherence. Together with comprehension, explanation provides for a *va-et-vient* process between the object's structure and an embodying totalizing structure.

Cf. comprehension.

FALSE CONSCIOUSNESS/Verdinglichung des Bewusstseins/ La fausse conscience

Heidegger's use of this term, which he puts in quotation marks, is comparable to Lukács's use of reification. For Heidegger, though, the problem of false consciousness is on the ontic level (that of the positive sciences), but it can only be illuminated by an ontological investigation which has nothing to do with science. For Lukács the problem is on the level of science but is also an intrinsically philosophical problem (Heidegger would say ontological here). The two levels are not opposed to each other, then, but are related dialectically.

FORMS

Goldmann says that forms, as Lukács speaks about them in *The Soul and the Forms*, are equivalent to his own concept of significant structures, only with the difference that these latter, rather than being idealistic or Neo-Kantian in origin, are dialecticized, placed within history by being concretely attached to collective subjects.

FUNCTION

A crucial term in Goldmann's genetic structuralism since it indissolubly links structures to the specific historical praxis of collective subjects. Structures are significant in relation to their function, and it is in their function that structures are seen in their historicity and genesis.

Cf. genetic structuralism, significant structure.

GENETIC STRUCTURALISM

Goldmann's particular model of the sociology of totality (synthesized from Jean Piaget, Lukács and the young Marx) which allows for the study of the genesis of structures and their function, as an essential aspect in interpreting their meaning. Thus, they are seen in their historical concreteness by which both the synchronic and diachronic levels are methodologized.

Cf. function, significant structure.

INAUTHENTIC/uneigentlich/inauthentique

The condition of Being-there in the state of oblivion, when the individual loses sight of his being-free-for-death. In such a state Being-there is lost in the Other, the one, according to Heidegger.

Cf. authentic, Being-there.

LEBENSPHILOSOPHIE

Life philosophy as elaborated by W. Dilthey. One proceeds to study life as a whole in order to understand individual experiences.

LIFE

Goldmann makes the following distinctions:
The life/*Das* Leben/*La* vie, which stands for the perspective of authentic Being-there; the *Life*/das *Leben*/la *Vie*, which stands for the perspective of inauthentic Being-there in its false consciousness.

NEGATIVE DIALECTIC

This conception of dialectic is the subject of T. Adorno's *Negative Dialektik* (Frankfurt am Main: Suhrkamp Verlag, 1966) and is linked to his critical theory where theory is freed from its reliance on praxis in order for the consciousness to effect a radical, totally negative, denunciation of praxis. Totality, then, is a completely negative category for which Goldmann was to accuse Adorno of dualism and voluntarism.

Cf. critical consciousness, truth content.

OBJECTIVE POSSIBILITY

The external situation of a class which limits its field of possibility with regard to thought and action. The mental structures of a class also circumscribe its theoretico-practical field of possibility. The objective possibility of a class determines its possible consciousness and inversely, according to Lukács. The two are inseparable.

Cf. possible consciousness.

OBJECTIVITY/Gegenstandsstruktur/L'objectivité

This Lukácsian category refers to the structuration of an object within a specific problematic. The object is never a mere given, but must be understood in its genesis, according to its structuring subject. There is no absolute objectivity in itself, according to Lukács, only the structuration of the object by a subject who is also within a greater historical totality.

ONE/Das Man/On

Heidegger's term for the 'they', the averageness of in-authentic Being-there as lived by Others. Goldmann compares this condition with that described by Lukács's reification.

Cf. inauthentic, reification.

ONTIC/ontisch/ontique

The domain of knowledge relegated by Heidegger to the positive sciences, the study of facts and technology, in other words. For him the ontic is a separate sphere from the ontological and is less fundamental, it not being concerned with the Being of Being-there which is an ontological entity, but only with the Being of entities other than Being-there.

Cf. ontological, ontology.

ONTOLOGICAL/ontologisch/ontologique

The domain of knowledge specific to philosophy, according to Heidegger. The ontological and the ontic are two separate spheres of knowledge.

Cf. ontology.

ONTOLOGY/Ontologie/L'ontologie

The science of Being as methodologized by phenomenology. The question of Being is described by analysing Being-there and is inseparable from the latter.

Cf. Being, phenomenology, Being-there.

PERSONALISM

Heidegger, in *Being and Time*, cites Scheler's philosophy as personalistic, i.e., the person is considered to be the unity of his lived experiences (Er-lebens) and not a substance or a thing existing behind or beyond such experiences. The person, then, is not an object, but is his experiences.

PHENOMENOLOGY

Heidegger's methodology in *Being and Time*, taken from E. Husserl. This is a method which explains the *how* of research but does not specify the subject matter. The method is 'to let that which shows itself be seen from itself in the very way in which it shows itself from itself'. Its axiom is: 'To the things themselves!'

POSITIVISM

An approach to reality · which privileges facts or data as givens by declaring them to be immediately intelligible without the need to refer them to a constituting subject or to an all-embracing totality. Positivism in the human sciences, for example, can be the application of the methodology of the physico-chemical sciences to the study of society or the individual. The researcher is considered as a neutral observer in relation to his object of study because implied is a subject-object dualism which results in the separation of theory from praxis and value judgments from judgments of fact.

POSSIBLE CONSCIOUSNESS/zugerechnetes Bewusstsein/ La conscience possible

The maximum adequation to reality possible by the collective consciousness of a class (keeping in mind it might never realize it) without it being led to abandon its significant structuration. It is the field, calculated by the researcher, within which the possible responses of a class can vary without there being an essential modification of its collective consciousness in its orientation toward a global structuration of society. This is a crucial category of *History and Class Consciousness* and is linked with the categories real consciousness and objective possibility. Lukács uses it to explain the relation between the individual subject on the level of social class and the limits of his social praxis.

Cf. real consciousness, objective possibility.

PRACTICO-INERT/practico-inerte

A term from Sartre's *La Critique de la raison dialectique* which describes that which is non-meaningful and non-dialectical, the external condition limiting a subject's freedom. The individual is not in a position of interaction, but only reaction, with this reality. This category is comparable to Heidegger's *Vorhandenheit*.

Cf. Presence-at-hand (Vorhandenheit).

PRESENCE-AT-HAND/Vorhandenheit/étant là (le monde comme donné)

Heidegger's term for the world as given, as present, and the consciousness of the subject must simply comprehend it. Such materials as wood, minerals, or water are included here, those things not needing to be produced. These entities are beyond what is readiness-to-hand (*Zuhandenheit*) and are more basic as well. There is no equivalent category in Lukács, praxis being comparable to *Zuhandenheit*.

Cf. readiness-to-hand.

READINESS-TO-HAND/Zuhandenheit/La manipulabilité

The instrumentality or manipulability of entities in relation to some purpose given them by the subject. Entities in such instances take their definition from their function, their usability. With this interactionist aspect involved, Goldmann likens the category to Lukács's use of praxis.

REAL CONSCIOUSNESS

The term given by Lukács to the rich and multiple content, the immediate empirical state, of the individual consciousnesses making up a class or group which is more or less coherent in its tendencies, depending upon the historical self-awareness of the individuals and the conditions for this self-awareness. It is the complement of possible consciousness.

Cf. possible consciousness.

REIFICATION

This category from *History and Class Consciousness* is Lukács's elaboration of Marx's term 'commodity fetishism', treated only cursorily in *Capital*. The term describes the psychic structure of men living in a capitalist society where the economic sector dominates over the other sectors. In such a society the relations of production, characterized by exchange value, determine interhuman relations as well, so that human beings are reduced to the merchandise they produce. The category of totality is lost sight of, qualitative values are transformed into quantitative ones, and people are reduced to the status of mere spectators.

REPETITION/Wiederholen/La répétition

Heidegger's term for resoluteness which, coming back to itself and handing itself down, becomes the repetition of a possibility of existence that has come down to Being-there. This is neither a mechanical process on the part of Being-there, nor is it a simple repetition of a past event. Rather, repetition means to return to the past and recover its *possibilities*, thus, the handing down.

RESOLUTE-DECISION/beschliessen (to decide), entschliessen (to resolve)/La décision-résolute

According to Heidegger, the concept describes the ontological decision revealed in the existentiality of Being-there in which this latter is called forth from its lostness in the 'they'. It is the individual's decision to repeat the life of a past hero, thereby entering into an authentic being-with in the community of a people (destiny). Only by authentically Being-their-Selves in resoluteness can people be-with one another authentically.

Cf. destiny, being-with.

SIGNIFICANT STRUCTURE

All structures are significant in so far as they have a functional necessity with relation to a particular subject. To discover this function, one must place the structure within an englobing vaster structure which involves revealing its genesis within the praxis of a collective subject as well.

Cf. function, transindividual subject.

SPATIALIZATION

This Bergsonian concept Joseph Gabels compares to Lukács's false consciousness (see J. Gabels's *La Fausse conscience*, Paris: Editions de Minuit, 1962), though Goldmann objects to the identification. According to Gabels, authentic consciousness, de-reification, is essentially an act of temporalization. Goldmann, however, maintains that for Lukács it is the absence of praxis (spatialization) which results in reification.

STRUCTURALISM

By this term Goldmann means to include those French thinkers such as Lévi-Strauss, L. Althusser, R. Barthes, Foucault and Lacan, who in studying structures, eliminate becoming, praxis and the generating subject from their methodology. According to Goldmann, they eliminate a structure's significance by ignoring its historical function as revealed in the social praxis of collective subjects (social classes, groups), that is, structures for them are viewed statically and synchronically. Goldmann's own genetic structuralism is a correction of this approach (ultra-rationalistic) in so far as it re-establishes the epistemological circle and the dialectical unity of the subject-object, and theory and praxis.

Cf. genetic structuralism, epistemological circle, dialectic.

TOTALITY/Totalität/La totalité

Refers to the entire determinate social process made up of the ensemble of relations between the classes (relative totalities) of a society and their relationship with nature. Totality is a dynamic whole always in the process of structuration and destructuration, according to the inter-action of social classes with each other. There is no perspective outside of this totality, nor can elements within it be understood without dialectically referring them to it, and inversely. This category, elaborated in *History and Class Consciousness*, is at the centre of both Lukács's and Goldmann's thought. Goldmann here compares it to Heidegger's category of Being.

TRANSCENDENTAL EGO

A philosophical construction representing consciousness in general over and against the world and history, with the *a priori* privileging of the former. The result, contrary to the empirical subject of the positive sciences, favours theory over praxis and the subject over the object, though both the transcendental ego and the empirical subject of posi-tivism imply a dualistic vision of the world. Against this dualism Goldmann positions the transindividual (collective) subject, as it is found in *History and Class Consciousness*.

TRANSINDIVIDUAL SUBJECT

A social class or group made up of individuals finding themselves in the same socio-economic conditions. Contrary to the transcendental subject, this plural subject, rather than being outside of and prior to history, is within it and helps to make it, thus the dialectical and circular relation between the subject and object, theory and praxis, and value judgments and judgments of fact. It is men, the 'we', who are at the origin of ideas and actions, collective subjects bound to collective praxis within the totality of the praxis of other classes and groups constituting the human community. According to Lukács and Goldmann, and contrary to Heidegger, it is at this level that transforming action becomes objectively possible and at this level of conceptualization that one can think of forming an authentic totality.

TRUTH CONTENT

Adorno's term (see his *Ästhetische Theorie*, Frankfurt am Main: Suhrkamp-Verlag, 1970) for the negative power in a work of art, usually embodied in its form as the presence of an absence, which is only seizable by the critical consciousness of the philosopher. The truth content is not reducible to an idea but is only apparent as a negative critique of reality, as a radical break with it. This break, however, implies the presence of a utopian non-being, a kind of possibility evident only through the radical protest of the work of art. The truth content of a work is not an abstraction separable from it, nor is it pure immanence; it exists indirectly in the work's structure. For Goldmann this position is not valid since there is no way to criticize the critical consciousness which seems to have an absolute and subjective status.

Cf. critical consciousness, negative dialectic.

WORLD VISION

The ensemble of mental categories of a social class tending toward a global organization of society. Such a perspective, based on the collective praxis of a class in relationship to the other classes making up society, is eminently concrete, particular and dialectical. Though Goldmann takes the category proximately from the early Lukács, *The Soul and the Forms* and *The Theory of the Novel*, he dialecticizes it with those transindividual subjects who generate them, thus removing the term from Lukács's Neo-Kantian and idealistic context.

Part 1

Introduction to Lukács
and Heidegger

(written in August 1970)

Introduction to Lukács and Heidegger

The *rapprochement* today of two famous philosophers, who are usually placed in separate contexts, may surprise the reader. Lukács, having adopted the communist position as early as 1917, and having been ignored since the end of the First World War by bourgeois university philosophy, which only began to show an interest in him again as a Marxist philosopher from around 1950, seems to be situated in an entirely different intellectual context from that of Heidegger, a representative figure of existentialism. For the average university graduate, the very most a book on Heidegger and Lukács can do is contrast two autonomous and antagonistic philosophers.

In this work, I propose to show, on the contrary, that this is an illusion born of an 'ahistorical' view which projects the present situation into the past, a situation which is itself difficult to understand if one is not situated in a genetic perspective. I will also try to take the opposite view from the customary perspective, going back to the situation of European, and in particular German, philosophy at the beginning of the century, to show how, on the basis of a new problematic first represented by Lukács, and later on by Heidegger, the contemporary situation was slowly created. I would add that this perspective will also enable us to display a whole range of elements common to both philosophers, which are not very visible at first sight, but which nevertheless constitute the common basis on which undeniable antagonisms are elaborated.

In fact, it was at the beginning of this century, around two

German universities, Heidelberg and Freiburg, and within what is usually called 'the south-west German philosophical school', that a change was effected which was to prove the source of the principal European philosophical currents of the first half of the twentieth century. This change was to take two directions: on the one hand, the birth of phenomenology and, from it, existentialism, and on the other hand, via phenomenology and existentialism, the birth of dialectical Marxism, with Lukács and the Lukácsian school.

The difficulty in carrying out such a study and the apparently unexpected and paradoxical character of this perspective are due to the fact that by rallying to Marxism around 1917, by returning to Hungary and by becoming people's commissar in the government of Béla Kun, G. Lukács left his original milieu and joined a trend which, for the sociologist and historian of philosophy, would seem to have nothing in common with university philosophy, and to be entering a tradition and a dynamic entirely opposed to the latter. It was — after 1917 — mainly in relation to Lenin, Rosa Luxemburg, and possibly Kautsky and Austro-Marxism, that the idea gradually took hold of considering Lukács's work as an important turning-point in the history of Marxist thought.

In reality, and despite appearances, Marxist philosophy and university philosophy, both expressions of different sectors of the same global society, have never been radically separate. The two were always in communication with one another despite prejudices and a show of hostility. In fact, the young Marx and Engels developed within the Neo-Hegelianism of the left which was bound to the revolutionary crises of the years 1830—48 and, even though they continued their work after the collapse of progressive Neo-Hegelianism, which followed the defeat of the revolution, their disciples — Kautsky, Plekhanov, Bernstein and even Lenin — transformed their thought as early as the close of the nineteenth century, orienting it toward a positivism quite close in some ways to university positivism and critical philosophy.

The evolution from Marx to Bernstein, Kautsky and Plekhanov is quite homologous to that which caused the German university philosophy of Hegel and the Neo-

Hegelians to pass, via Schopenhauer and Haym, to Neo-Kantianism and university positivism. Although for political reasons, Marxists could not enter the university before 1918, the entry of Marxists into the German-speaking universities did not involve any upheaval: their contribution was limited to the creation of a small number of courses scarcely different from those already in existence.

It was in relation to this positivism, both university and Marxist, that the beginning of the century was to produce a rather profound break. Consequently, one can understand why the same representative figure of this break, G. Lukács, was able to provoke it both at the level of university teaching and, later, at the level of Marxist thought. That is why, if we wish to establish the facts from their origin, it will be necessary, at least at the outset, to forget G. Lukács's later evolution and situate him in the pleiad of the great university figures living at Heidelberg and Freiburg at the beginning of this century.

In the second half of the nineteenth century and up until around 1910, German philosophy was dominated by the Neo-Kantian schools, the two most important being that of Marburg, oriented toward logic and the theory of the sciences, and that of Heidelberg, oriented, above all, toward the historical sciences. Each of them had a review which played a leading role in German philosophical life: *Kant-Studien* at Marburg and *Logos* at Heidelberg (the equivalents of the *Revue de Métaphysique et de Morale* and the *Revue philosophique* in France). Each of these schools also had three leaders in succession who were, respectively: H. Cohen, F. Natorp and E. Cassirer at Marburg; W. Windelbandt, H. Rickert and E. Lask at Heidelberg. Lask died in 1915 and Rickert after Hitler seized power.

At the beginning of this century, the historical orientation of the Heidelberg school brought the philosophers of that university into contact with the psychologists and sociologists of the same city, among whom the most important were Max Weber and W. Sombart. At the same time, at the neighbouring university of Freiburg, a philosophical turning-point, the importance of which was less noticeable at the outset than it was to become later on, emerged with E.

3

Husserl's creation of phenomenology through his yearly publication, *Jahrbuch für philosophie und phäno-menologischee Forschung.* Among the young intellectuals who gathered around these centres, closely collaborating with Lask and influenced by Husserl, five names were later to emerge as particularly important: K. Jaspers, G. Lukács, Broder, Christiansen and also, though more marginally, Ernst Bloch.

It is not very easy to define the philosophical turning-point which was to emerge during the first years of the century in what we might call, for the sake of simplification, not the 'school' — as is usual — but the south-west German philosophical 'milieu', which was to have a decisive influence on twentieth-century European philosophical thought. This is particularly the case because it is not a matter of a linear evolution, but of the convergence of a whole series of lines pointing in the same direction, merging, crossing one another and diverging, to end up finally in two great philosophical schools: existentialism and dialectical materialism. Even while writing this, I am nevertheless aware of having simplified such a development to a degree bordering on distortion. It goes without saying that neither existentialism nor dialectical materialism were born between 1900—30 at Heidelberg or at Freiburg. The origins of existentialism date back at least to Kierkegaard, and dialectical thought was of course first systematically elaborated by Hegel, to take on a materialist form with Marx and Engels. And yet, between Kierkegaard, Hegel and Marx on the one hand, and the existentialist and Marxist works of Lukács on the other (*The Soul and the Forms*, 1911, and *History and Class Consciousness*, 1923), runs a long period of positivist thought which has dominated western European philosophy, so that the appearance of these two books must be regarded as ,a veritable renaissance. In this sense, and with this reservation, it is not incorrect to say that between 1910 and 1925 a true philosophical turning-point occurred, which resulted in the creation of existentialism and contemporary dialectical materialism.

It should also be pointed out that, although it was G. Lukács who initiated both these vectors, his rediscovery of dialectical Marxism occurred after he left Heidelberg to join the government of Béla Kun in Hungary. Furthermore, the appearance of *History and Class Consciousness*, that major event in the evolution of Marxist thought, would scarcely be conceivable if it were abstracted from the total philosophical problematic developed by Lukács's writings between 1911 and 1923.

Basically, if one tries to describe even very schematically the intellectual networks upon which we propose to shed some light here, first of all a line must be envisaged describing Lukács's progress in first creating existentialist philosophy by integrating certain ideological elements gathered from Dilthey, Simmel, Lask and Kierkegaard, in order to orient himself later on towards the Hegelianism of the *Theory of the Novel* and the Marxism of *History and Class Consciousness*; a second line, brought to light by Roberto Miguelez, who has shown how, in *History and Class Consciousness*, Lukács integrates certain important elements of Husserl's thought; finally, a third line which starts from *History and Class Consciousness* and *The Soul and the Forms* and ends in a much more Kierkegaardian synthesis in Heidegger's *Being and Time*. Finally, around this central kernel and starting from it, the flowering of phenomenology and existentialism was to develop and establish a significant place for itself in European thought, as well as in the socialist utopianism of Ernst Bloch. Of this extremely complex network, we propose to study here only a partial, but particularly important, sector: the relation between the thought of Lukács and Heidegger's famous work *Being and Time*.

We have just said that phenomenology and existentialism constituted a fundamental break with traditional thought. What were the basic elements of this break? To begin, one seems to me to be of particular importance: the traditional philosophy of the progressive and revolutionary bourgeoisie, as well as that of the bourgeoisie in power, had radically separated the *subject* of consciousness and the action of the *object* which both were concerned with. On the one hand, there was the knowing and the acting man, the scholar, the engineer, the political leader and on the other hand, confronting them, the natural and social world which they had to understand and transform. On the basis of this duality, a whole range of other alternatives unquestionably developed: determinism and freedom, power and humanism, knowledge and morality, synchronism and diachronism, etc., which I need not dwell on here; but already the subject/object dualism was difficult to defend. If the subject's consciousness and action are subjected to the causal action of the world in which they are taking place, it is very difficult to safeguard their rational and significant character, which is oriented towards an end. If, inversely, one keeps the absolute and free character of the beginning of the subject's consciousness and action, it is very difficult to safeguard the determinist character, ordered and deprived of proper meaning, of the universe in which the action of the subject constantly intervenes. There is a difficulty here which all the philosophers of individualism have encountered from Descartes and the major Cartesians, Leibniz, Malebranche and Spinoza to the Encyclopaedists and Diderot, a difficulty which Kant thought he had resolved by making a radical separation between the intelligible world and the world of experience, which Marx made an object of sarcastic criticism in the third of his *Theses on Feuerbach* and with which thinkers such as Lévi-Strauss and Marcuse still clash today, a difficulty which only found its solution in the dialectical thought of Hegel and Marx. This solution — which had been ignored by university philosophy during the entire second half of the nineteenth century — was taken up again by Husserl, Lukács and Heidegger. Man is not *opposite* the world which he tries to understand and upon which he acts, but *within* this world which he is a part of, and there is no radical break between the meaning he is trying to find or introduce into the universe and that which he is trying to find or introduce into his own existence. This meaning, common to both individual and collective human life, common as much to humanity as, ultimately, to the universe, is called *history*.

Starting from this common basis, one can distinguish two

6

fundamental differences between the theses of Lukács and Husserl: they deal with what can be called transcendental idealism. Despite everything, there is, for Husserl, an absolute beginning and this beginning is idealist in character. If the subject exists *only* in relation to the world, if its consciousness is always consciousness-of, Husserl, despite everything, accords a constitutive function — that is, a primacy — to the subject in relation to the world and, since this constitution can in no way be attributed to the empirical subject, to you or to me, he has been obliged to keep the transcendental subject of the Neo-Kantians. Needless to say, this philosophical monstrosity could in no instance have a collective character. It is therefore understandable why the principal Neo-Kantians, notably Natorp, at first had the impression that there was no difference between Husserl's thought and their own philosophy. In fact, these differences were quite considerable: the transcendental subject of the Neo-Kantians constitutes three strictly separate and complementary conceptual worlds, whereas the transcendental subject of Husserl constitutes the world as a whole and, within this latter, a considerable number of different domains corresponding to regional ontologies and, notably, the *Lebenswelt,* the world of immediate daily life. Nevertheless, Husserlian idealism kept the transcendental subject of Kant and the Neo-Kantians, the sole possibility of reconciling the ontological primacy of the subject with the definition of man as a 'being-in-the-world', a transcendental subject which Hegel and Marx had already renounced and which the great existentialist thinkers, the young Lukács (and, of course, the later Marxist Lukács), Heidegger, Jaspers, and Sartre were to renounce in their turn.

There, then, is the first fundamental bond between Lukács and Heidegger: continued from the Hegelian tradition, the rejection of the transcendental subject, the conception of man as inseparable from the world which he is a part of, the definition of his place in the universe as historicity. Let us specify further that if *Sein und Zeit* is composed of two complementary, but yet distinct, parts, the problem of being and the fundamental analysis of being-there, the majority of the ideas which Heidegger has in common with Lukács are found in the latter in two different works: the theory of limit, and authenticity as bound to this limit, in *The Soul and the Forms*; the analysis of totality (the question of Being, for Heidegger), the unity of theory and practice, the practical character of the first, the theoretical character of the second, and finally, the problem of meaning, in *History and Class Consciousness*.

Finally, it is also necessary to emphasize the differences which put the two philosophies in opposition to each other, but on this common foundation. Also, because of these differences, where Lukács sees an inevitable choice between the tragic philosophy of the all or nothing and the Marxist philosophy of history, Heidegger proposes a synthesis in a romantic philosophy of history.

These differences, above all, bear upon the fact that for Heidegger the historical subject is the individual whereas Lukács, tracing in it the authentic tradition of Hegel and Marx, conceives of history as the action of the transindividual subject and, in particular, of social classes. Two other equally important differences result from this major difference.

First, for Lukács history is the result of the action of all men and is made under a global 'vector', thus capable of being ranged under the category of progress or reaction, of increase or decrease of knowledge or freedom. On the other hand, for Heidegger the concept of progress is deprived of meaning, history only having two dimensions, authenticity and inauthenticity; the existential (the equivalent of the Lukácsian 'category'), which directs it, being that of repetition (of authenticity on the part of individuals of the élite who make history) and inevitable catastrophe (not made explicit by Heidegger, but implicit, because it is the empirical expression of the oblivion of authenticity, of the relapse into the inauthentic), since it must occur in the best of cases at the death of the élite individuals, the philosophers, poets, or heads of state.

The third difference also results from the distinction between the individual and the collective subject: historical action being, for both Lukács and Heidegger, inaccessible to positivist knowledge (ontology, for Heidegger, in *Sein und*

Zeit), for Lukács, because everything that men do has a historical character, there could be no difference between the human sciences and philosophy, both being the knowledge of the historical subject. For Heidegger, on the other hand, for whom historical action is the privilege of élitists to the exclusion of the masses, it is possible to have a positive and non-philosophical sociology of the latter, the historical subjects alone — the statesman, the poet and the philosopher — being dependent on ontological comprehension.

In other words, for both Lukács and Heidegger the knowledge of history and historical action could only be philosophical (or, which is the same thing, ontological), since positivist knowledge is reserved for everything which takes place in the world outside this action. But for Heidegger, as only a certain number of élite individuals are creators of history, only their behaviour escapes positivist science, which can embrace the domain of the natural sciences just as well as sociology or the psychology of the masses who live inauthentically. For Lukács, on the contrary, since history is the result of the actions of all men, the frontier between the positivist and the philosophical sciences does not lie between the comprehension of the creators and the knowledge of the rest of the natural and social universe, but between the physico-chemical and the human sciences, since the latter cannot be scientific without being philosophical. Finally, the historical action of élites could only be, for Heidegger, a sporadic repetition of returns from the inauthenticity of the *One* to authenticity, a necessarily limited repetition (this could only occur through the lives of creative individuals), which must inevitably finish, by means of oblivion and relapse, in the *One*, until the following repetition. For Lukács, on the contrary, history is the action of all men which, through contradictions, particular interests, the egoism of social groups, and notably social classes, is oriented toward the growth of knowledge and freedom in relation to which it either progresses or regresses.

Before broaching an analysis of the thought of the two philosophers, it is still necessary to say a few words about the problem of language. If the relationship between the thought of Lukács and that of Heidegger has not been noticed by historians of philosophy for more than fifty years, it is, among other things, because there is a radical difference of terminology between them, and identical — or at least highly related — things are expressed in an entirely different way by each of them. This difference, moreover, is not accidental; it results, at least in part, from the fact that Heidegger (for whom ontology is radically separated from the positive sciences of which it only constitutes the foundation) attempts to construct a rigorously coherent system and give an absolutely univocal meaning to different terms which he has created throughout his development. On the contrary, Lukács, for whom the social sciences and philosophy are inseparable, must take into account the triple dimension resulting from the demand for the coherence of the system, the description of empirical facts, and the maintenance of scientific terminology present whenever there is no absolute necessity to modify it. One reason explaining the difference of terminology is the fact that Heidegger is writing for a university audience accustomed not only to accept, but even to admire, rigorous linguistic structures, whereas Lukács is speaking to a Marxist audience, to trade union groups and to party workers to whom he must communicate a series of rather unfamiliar and difficult ideas. In this situation it is natural for him to concentrate mainly on the necessity to make himself understood, by trying as much as possible to keep to customary Marxist terminology.

Consequently, in order to express approximate, at times nearly identical, ideas, Lukács will speak about 'totality' where Heidegger will use the word 'Being'; about 'man' where Heidegger will create the term 'Being-there'; about 'praxis' where Heidegger will use the term *'Zuhandenheit'* (approximately: 'manipulability'). Lukács will vary his periphrases little to indicate the passive perception of reality, either in daily perception or in the pretension to make of it a purely objective theorization, where Heidegger will use *'Vorhandenheit'*, that which is there, before the hand, presenting itself, then, as independent of all praxis. It is obvious that the use of the words *Zuhandenheit* and *Vorhandenheit* is extremely suggestive in indicating the common element of their position and opposition, and that we have here an evocative verbal creation, which is nevertheless unusable in a Marxist work. For although the word *Vorhanden* is current German usage and universally understandable, the word *Zuhanden*, on the contrary, is — in the sense Heidegger gives it — an artificial creation which no serious Marxist could substitute for the universally accepted term 'praxis', which fulfils its function perfectly. Likewise, it is hard to imagine a Marxist book in which 'man' and 'subject' would be replaced by *'Dasein'*, 'Being-there'.

It should also be added that this terminological difference, which can be overcome by respectively translating the developments of each thinker into the terminology of the other, gives rise at times to theoretical analyses, the least one can say about which is that they risk creating confusion. This is the case, for example, with the primary problem of the relations of the subject and the object.

I have already said that the dialectical thought of Hegel and Marx, as well as later on the philosophical turning-point in the south-west German milieu in the years 1920—30, were largely born of the demand to overcome the opposition between the subject and the object of action which has been the basis of Western philosophy since the development of rationalism and empiricism, that is to say — according to where one situates the break — since Greek antiquity, after Plato and Aristotle, or since St Thomas and, in any case, since Descartes. To assert the theoretically unacceptable character of this opposition, Hegel, Marx and Lukács adopted the formula — which appears explicit enough to me — of the 'identity of the subject and the object'. It is also true that, in order to criticize this opposition, the formula also uses the two terms which are both distinct and, in their current sense, opposed. By replacing 'totality' with *'Sein'* ('Being'), and 'subject' with *'Dasein'* ('Being-there'), Heidegger creates a terminology which undoubtedly has the advantage of expressing, in the very structure of the formula, both the identity and the relative difference of the two concepts. He is, then, able to criticize (but apparently only in a justified manner) any philosophy which still uses the terms 'subject'-'object' as continuing in the wake of traditional ontology in relation to which his own thought would constitute a radical break. In reality, there is not much difference between the assertion that 'Being-there' poses the question of the meaning of 'Being' and that to pose it, he must also ask what his own 'Being' is — the 'Being' of 'Being-there' — and the assertion that the subject poses the question of the meaning of history, and that this question presupposes that of its own existence in so far as historical being and part of this historical reality which constitutes the object of the question. It should also be added that, if the question of the meaning of 'Being' or history presupposes the question of the meaning of life and human actions, the converse is no less true. There is no absolute priority of the subject, of 'Being-there' in relation to the object, to totality, to 'Being', nor inversely.

A word more on the two central concepts of the two philosophies: that of *reification* and *false consciousness* in the terminology of Lukács; that of *Vorhandenheit*, the *One*, and *inauthenticity* in that of Heidegger.

Starting from the famous analysis of commodity fetishism developed by Marx in the first chapter of *Capital*, Lukács, by substituting the word 'reification' for the Marxist term, had developed a general theory of false consciousness to which he dedicated half his work and in which he showed how this reification, bound to market production, finally led to the different forms of false consciousness and to the perception of the external world as a pure object only capable of being known and modified, to what Heidegger would call *Vorhandenheit*, which is found at the basis of every objectivist interpretation and, especially, all metaphysics as *theory* of being.

Heidegger, who is not of course interested in the different historically and socially localized aspects of the variations of consciousness and recognizes only radical dualisms (authentic/inauthentic, science/ontology, *Vorhandenheit/Zuhandenheit*, etc.), will only tell us that the spontaneous consciousness tends to understand 'Being-there' (man) on the basis of the world as *Vorhanden*, which is none other than the Marxist and Lukácsian analysis which tells us that, in reification, human reality and social facts are understood as things. Needless to say, Heidegger does not look for any historical basis for this illusion. Starting from there, one understands the character inherent to this thought which is both sincere and, despite everything, hardly justified, in the assertion which he puts at the beginning and the end of *Sein und Zeit* as a sort of framework, to justify his claim to originality. It is an assertion in which, without naming Lukács, he criticizes his analysis of reification by telling us that it has a socio-historical status which must be onto-logically justified, whereas the Lukácsian thesis is precisely that there could be no ontological basis outside the know-ledge of society and history.[1]

Yet, whatever the position admitted to, the existence of these two passages, their place in the book (at the beginning and the end of the analysis), the use in 1927 of the words 'reification of consciousness' between quotation marks, whereas the work of Lukács had developed this concept as a central element of his philosophy as early as 1923, seems to us unquestionably to indicate the intellectual context in which *Sein und Zeit* is situated, the interlocutor with whom Heidegger was carrying on a discussion and the place he wanted to occupy in relation to him.

It should also be added that the fact that he does not name Lukács (at a time when Lukács was withdrawing from all public intellectual activity for reasons of party discipline, had repudiated his work and was unable to reply), whereas he did name Husserl, Scheler, and Bergson, has created a confusion which, on Heidegger's part, was perhaps not entirely involun-tary.

If we now begin the analysis of the philosophical system presented in *Sein und Zeit*, we ascertain that the first question which, according to Heidegger, must be asked of philosophy is that of the meaning of Being, that this question could only be asked starting from a privileged being, the one who poses the question of Being-there, starting from man. Next, Heidegger declares that the answer which finally emerges from his analysis is that the nature of Being is its historicity, and the nature of Being-there is its temporality, constituted by the possibility of living according to two different modes: that of authenticity and that of inauthenticity, which appear not as properties but as possibilities of the latter. Finally, the comprehension of this problematic as a whole presumes a phenomenological ontology which radically breaks with natural and spontaneous knowledge, because Being-there tends to comprehend the surrounding reality spontaneously as objective reality, as *Vorhanden*, and to comprehend itself not starting from its own possibilities, but from this objective reality, as an object similar to many others. Finally, a particularly important point, the ontological position of the problem of the meaning of Being and Being-there, when defined from their possibilities, ends in having Being-there understood as being *in* a world and not as a being who possesses a world or who has a world opposite it, which would be to remain on the level of traditional ontology.

If we now try to analyse the preface of Lukács's *History and Class Consciousness* more closely, we will have an idea both of the close relationship and the radical difference between the two thinkers.

Like Heidegger, Lukács in his preface announces a total break with traditional science and metaphysics. Yet, it goes without saying, he designates the valid method as dialectical and not as ontological or metaphysical. With the aid of a quotation from Hegel, he poses the problem of terminology and forestalls Heidegger's objection to those who still use the concepts of subject and object:

> While dwelling on such shortcomings I should perhaps point out to the reader unfamiliar with dialectics one difficulty inherent in the nature of dialectical method relating to the definition of concepts and terminology. It is of the essence of dialectical method that concepts which are false in their abstract onesidedness are later transcended (zur Aufhebung gelangen). The process of transcendence makes it inevitable that we should operate with these one-sided, abstract and false concepts. These concepts acquire their true meaning less by definition than by their function as aspects that are then transcended in the totality. Moreover, it is even more difficult to establish fixed meanings for concepts in Marx's improved

version of the dialectic than in the Hegelian original. For if concepts are only the intellectual forms of historical realities then these forms, one-sided, abstract and false as they are, belong to the true unity as genuine aspects of it. Hegel's statements about this problem of terminology in the preface to the *Phenomenology* are thus even more true than Hegel himself realised when he said: 'Just as the expressions "unity of subject and object", of "finite and infinite", of "being and thought", etc., have the drawback that "object" and "subject" bear the same meaning as when *they exist outside that unity*, so that within the unity they mean something other than is implied by their expressions: so, too, falsehood is not, *qua* false, any longer a moment of truth.' In the pure historicisation of the dialectic this statement receives yet another twist: in so far as the 'false' is an aspect of the 'true' it is both 'false' and 'non-false'. When the professional demolishers of Marx criticise his 'lack of conceptual rigour' and his use of 'image' rather than 'definitions', etc., they cut as sorry a figure as did Schopenhauer when he tried to expose Hegel's logical howlers in his Hegel critique. All that is proved is their total inability to grasp even the ABC of the dialectical method.[2]

In this same preface concerning the dialectical character of Marx's thought, Lukács underlined, as against positivist Marxism and notably the Neo-Kantian Marxist Vorländer, the central importance of the distinction that Marx constantly uses between the immediate and the mediate (a distinction which was to be developed in the work as the distinction between the part [immediate] and the totality [mediated]). Finally, a point which clearly illustrates the difference from Heidegger: Lukács excuses himself for having situated his work on an abstract and philosophical level while specifying, nevertheless, that the fact of discovering, or rediscovering, the dialectical method implies a total historicization of knowledge and action, and the demand to apply this method to the thought and the action of the subject, whose radical historicization is materialized in immediate and current problems.

One sees what the two methods have in common and where they are opposed. Being and history for Heidegger are situated on the ontological level, indeed the philosopher tells us frequently that participation in this ontology is indispensable for orienting oneself theoretically and practically

15

in daily life, for understanding oneself with one's possibilities as Being-there in the world. But none of this, i.e., science and politics, belongs to the domain of philosophy and ontology, even if this ontology permits one as an individual to assume positions in daily life as a scientist or a politician. Heidegger, who dissociates himself from science, does not, on the contrary, do so with regard to politics: by appealing to this ontology, he became one of the main heralds of national-socialism. Lukács, on the other hand, accepts no radical separation between the ontic and the ontological, between immediate problems and philosophy, and, if a primacy were possible here, he would accord it to the former. In fact, however, it is impossible to orient oneself at the scientific or the political level without inserting the immediate into the mediate, the part into the whole, the individual into the class, the class into society, and society into history. He is, therefore, obliged to approach philosophical problems from the basis of a concern to give valid responses to immediate problems and, since these problems — at the time he was writing, especially, where it was necessary to break with a long positive and dualist tradition of rationalism, empiricism, and even the thought of Kant — are particularly difficult, he was to become a philosopher and finish by writing, since Marx had not, the first major, truly philosophical work on dialectics.

I would add that outside the theoretical relationship and opposition which make up the object of the present work, there is an analogous relationship and opposition between the political stands of the two thinkers, that is to say, between Heidegger's relations with national-socialism and Lukács's with Stalinism. As is well-known, they both rallied to a political dictatorship on the basis of their respective global analyses of the meaning of history. And this adherence to the two different and opposed dictatorships had, in both cases, an analogous structure: for Heidegger as for Lukács, the meaning of totality (or Being) is manifested on the three equivalent levels of politics, philosophy, and art. From this starting point, their involvement could not be reduced to a servile adherence to the programme, demands, and orders of political leaders.

In this historical perspective, Heidegger situates himself at the same level as Hitler, Lukács at the same level as Stalin and, since they expressed the same totality on the level of consciousness, it goes without saying that they thought they understood the nature of the political fact better than the political leaders themselves. For Heidegger, anti-Semitism could only be regarded as a profound and regrettable error, the biological having no place in ontology and being totally unable to limit or further the Being-there's possibilities of choosing between the authentic and the inauthentic. On the other hand, Hitler could only be regarded as a charismatic leader, one of those exceptional men who discovered authenticity in the political dimension of history and who, like every 'repetition', had to finish with the return to the *One*, to the oblivion of authenticity, that means – politically – to catastrophe. For Lukács, Stalin and Stalinism were only a necessary, but transitory, phase of the Revolution: the Bonapartist phase, the function and meaning of which was to defend the essential attainments against outside, threatening, reactionary and powerful enemies.

Needless to say, neither Hitler nor Stalin were able to accept these positions: for the former, anti-Semitism constituted an essential element of his politics and, in particular, he promised his supporters lasting victory and a millenial kingdom. As for the Stalinists, far from accepting themselves as a transitory phase, they intended to achieve socialism in one country and to constitute a revolutionary force in the world. Likewise, the definition of Stalinism as Bonapartist, formulated by Trotsky as one of his most important ideas, was almost considered the supreme error in Stalinist circles.

It is clear that the two philosophers had almost identical difficulties with the two dictatorships to which they had rallied, and that on the other hand, after the fall of Hitlerism and Stalinism, they were probably among the few intellectuals who kept and defended their old positions, claiming specifically that they had understood the function of these dictatorships better than the majority of their partisans and leaders. (Did not Hitlerism in actual fact founder in catastrophe? Did not Stalinism in actual fact enable the immediate danger of Hitlerism to be overcome as well as the danger, virtual but nevertheless existent, of the encircling of the USSR and the anti-communist front of the major capitalist powers?)

If we now analyse the first essay of Lukács's book, 'What is Orthodox Marxism?', we notice that he begins by asserting that Marxist orthodoxy does not concern any of the master's concrete analyses. It concerns only his method, which consists in

> the scientific conviction that dialectical materialism is the road to truth and that its methods can be developed, expanded and deepened only along the lines laid down by its founders. It is the conviction, moreover, that all attempts to surpass or 'improve' it have led and must lead to over-simplification, triviality and eclecticism.[3]

Lukács asserts this attitude against those who oppose Marxism by demanding an 'objective' study of 'facts' and, in order to complete this position, he puts at the head of his study Marx's last thesis on Feuerbach: 'Philosophers have only *interpreted* the world in different ways; it should be *transformed*'. Throughout this study Lukács was to present the Marxist dialectical method as a radical break with the theory (according to him *unscientific*) which claims to make an objective study of reality by subjecting itself above all to empirical facts. Needless to say (this will become more and more obvious, moreover) this entire analysis is — at least in certain directions — analogous to the one Heidegger was to present in the phenomenological method and in the ontology based upon it, which conceives of the world as 'present' (*Vorhanden*), given, to a conscious subject which must simply comprehend it and act upon it. Whatever the differences may be — and they are great — there is a close relationship between Lukács's historical world of the close unity between theory and practice, and Heidegger's world in which Being-there is involved and in which reality has with it a relation of manipulability (*Zuhandenheit*).

'Dialectical materialism is a revolutionary dialectic.' It is this, Lukács tells us, which must be understood before one can approach all of its other constitutive elements:

> The issue turns on the question of theory and practice. And this not merely in the sense given it by Marx when he says in his first critique of Hegel that 'theory becomes a material force when it grips the

masses'. Even more to the point is the need to discover those features and definitions both of the theory and the ways of gripping the masses which convert the theory, the dialectical method, into a vehicle of revolution. We must extract the practical essence of the theory from the method and its relation to its object. . . .

In the same essay Marx clearly defined the conditions in which a relation between theory and practice becomes possible. 'It is not enough that thought should seek to realise itself; reality must also strive towards thought.' Or, as he expresses it in an earlier work: 'It will then be realised that the world has long since possessed something in the form of a dream which it need only take possession of consciously, in order to possess it in reality.'[4]

And Lukács concludes: 'Only when consciousness stands in such a relation to reality can theory and practice be united.'[5]

The last two quotations have a common element which places them in opposition to the first: the active factor. The initiation of revolutionary action in the subject which thinks and acts, in theory, but just as much and perhaps even primarily (in order to 'bend the staff'), in the direction of the object, of reality, which the subject is in the process of transforming. This idea is connected in certain ways to that which Heidegger was to develop four years later when he stated that the only really philosophical thought is that in which *Dasein*, Being-there, causes Being to speak and, therefore, finds its authentic relation with it. It is, nevertheless, opposed to the Heideggerian analysis to the extent that, for Heidegger, it is a question of a universally valid analysis which constitutes the foundation of history. Lukács, on the other hand, who is much more dialectical, develops this same assertion by adding a complement to it, i.e., the unity of theory and practice, the propensity of theory toward the world and of the world toward theory, is itself a historical fact the structure of which changes in the course of its development; the theorist could only validly analyse this unity to the extent in which he succeeds both in basing his comprehension of historical facts upon it — a thesis shared by Heidegger — and in basing this unity itself upon a concrete analysis of the aspect which the structuration of this unity grasps in an immediate way, *hic et nunc* — a task which

Heidegger would relegate to the ontic, excluding it from ontologico-philosophical reflection.

Let us add that one of the central ideas of the Lukácsian analysis — an idea he subsequently criticized and rejected — is that the historical epoch which began with the Bolshevik Revolution constituted the penultimate step toward a total and transparent identity between theory and practice. To put it more plainly, the book was written at a time when all the conditions of the socialist revolution obtained, save one: the raising of consciousness when this revolution was imminent. 'To be clear about the function of theory [revolutionary practice, L.G.] is also to understand its own basis, i.e. dialectical method.[6]

And, to indicate how radical his break was, Lukács criticized a book which at the time — and later on — functioned as a bible for vulgar and dogmatic Marxism: Engels's *Anti-Dühring*. Because, he tells us, whatever may be the enthusiasm with which Engels had asserted the fluid character, and the perpetual transformation, of concepts and the objects corresponding to them, the dynamic character of reality and its status as process, there is no mention of

> a continuous process of transition from one definition into the other . . . In consequence a one-sided and rigid causality must be replaced by interaction . . . But he does not even mention the most vital interaction; namely, the *dialectical relation between subject and object in the historical process*, let alone give it the prominence it deserves.[7]

The break with positivism concerns not only the rationalists, empiricists and Neo-Kantians, but also positivist pseudo-Marxism even including its most representative, most scientific, and most inspired work: the *Anti-Dühring*. Because, as Lukács says subsequently of this work,

> without this factor [the dialectical relation of the subject and object, L.G.] dialectics ceases to be revolutionary, despite attempts (illusory in the last analysis) to retain 'fluid' concepts. For it implies a failure to recognise that in all metaphysics the object remains untouched and unaltered so that thought remains contemplative and fails to become practical; while for the dialectical method the central problem is *to change reality*.
>
> If this central function of the theory is disregarded, the virtues of

forming 'fluid' concepts become altogether problematic: a purely 'scientific' matter. The theory might then be accepted or rejected in accordance with the prevailing state of science without any modification at all to one's basic attitudes, to the question of whether or not reality can be changed. Indeed, . . .it even reinforces the view that reality, with its 'obedience to laws', in the sense used by bourgeois, contemplative materialism and the classical economics with which it is so closely bound up, is impenetrable, fatalistic and immutable.[8]

Later, Lukács was to emphasize that all voluntarism — and we might add all theory of autonomous values — is only the other, subjective, face of one and the same coin, the complement to objectivist, fatalist and determinist theory, in a word the contemplation of reality.

The second paragraph is devoted to an analysis of the nature of empirical facts, which constitutes the central theme of positivist thought. Without going as far as contemporary epistemology perhaps, Lukács thinks that the very structure of the perceived object's invariance is a construction closely bound to the nature of the object and the praxis of the subject. He begins by observing that each fact is only given to us as an element of a broader context, fulfilling a certain function in that context, a function which alone decides its meaning and its pertinent or non-pertinent character for praxis. The facts are not pure data, an autonomous foundation starting from which theoretical and scientific analyses are constructed:

The blinkered empiricist will of course deny that facts can only become facts within the framework of a system — which will vary with the knowledge desired. He believes that every piece of data from economic life, every statistic, every raw event already constitutes an important fact. In so doing he forgets that however simple an enumeration of 'facts' may be, however lacking in commentary, it already implies an 'interpretation'. . . . More sophisticated opportunists would readily grant this despite their profound and instinctive dislike of all theory. They seek refuge in the methods of natural science, in the way in which science distills 'pure' facts and places them in the relevant contexts by means of observation, abstraction and experiment. They then oppose this ideal model of knowledge to the forced constructions of the dialectical method.[9]

To criticize this method, when it is a matter of the human or historical sciences, Lukács demonstrates:

(a) That capitalist society, by its very functioning, tends to give social facts a reified and quantitative aspect, analogous to the facts the natural sciences study, so that the utilization of these methods — which, apparently, are at times empirically confirmed — introduces *a priori* the fact that social reality naturally has, and must always maintain, a capitalist structure.

(b) That the application of these methods and the utilization of these research procedures methodologically eliminate the historical dimension of social facts, thus reinforcing the error resulting from the facts mentioned in the preceding paragraph.

(c) That in order to be able to be used, the methods for the establishment of facts (statistics, enquiries, etc.) necessitate rather a long period of time, so that their publication very often presents a state of affairs already overtaken by reality. This delay, relatively unimportant in a period of tranquility, can be a source of serious errors in the case of periods of rapid change.

With regard to point (a) above, as well as to the other two, Lukács says:

> In this way arise the 'isolated' facts, 'isolated' complexes of facts, separate, specialist disciplines (economics, law, etc.) whose very appearance seems to have done much to pave the way for such scientific methods. It thus appears extraordinarily 'scientific' to think out the tendencies implicit in the facts themselves [in the capitalist structure, L. G.] and to promote this activity to the status of science.

> By contrast, in the teeth of all these isolated and isolating facts and partial systems, dialectics insists on the concrete unity of the whole. Yet although it exposes these appearances for the illusions they are — albeit illusions necessarily engendered by capitalism — in this 'scientific' atmosphere it still gives the impression of being an arbitrary construction.

> The unscientific nature of this seemingly so scientific method consists, then, in its failure to see and take account of the *historical character* of the facts on which it is based.

The historical character of the 'facts' which science seems to have grasped with such 'purity' makes itself felt in an even more devastating manner. As the products of historical evolution they are involved in continuous change. But in addition they are also precisely in their objective structure the products of a definite historical epoch; namely, capitalism. . . .

This distinction is the first premise of a truly scientific study which in Marx's words 'would be superfluous if the outward appearance of things coincided with their essence'. Thus we must detach the phenomena from the form in which they are immediately given and discover the intervening links which connect them to their core, their essence. In so doing, we shall arrive at an understanding of their apparent form and see it as the form in which the inner core necessarily appears. . . . Only in this context which sees the isolated facts of social life as aspects of the historical process and integrates them in a *totality,* can knowledge of the facts hope to become knowledge of *reality.*[10]

This knowledge goes from the given to knowledge of concrete totality as the theoretical reproduction of reality: 'This concrete totality is by no means an unmediated datum for thought. "The concrete is concrete," Marx says, "because it is a synthesis of many particular determinants, i.e. a unity of diverse elements." '[11]

And, after having again criticized the 'syntheses' of idealism and vulgar materialism, Lukács ends the paragraph by recalling that

Marx's dictum: 'The relations of production of every society form a whole' is the methodological point of departure and the key to the *historical* understanding of social relations. All the isolated partial categories can be thought of and treated — in isolation — as something that is always present in every society. (If it cannot be found in a given society this is put down to 'chance' as the exception that proves the rule.) But the changes to which these individual aspects are subject give no clear and unambiguous picture of the real differences in the various stages of the evolution of society. These can really only be discerned in the context of the total historical process of their relation to society as a whole.[12]

The third paragraph begins with the observation that a thought centred upon the idea of totality, which apparently draws away from the immediate given, which apparently constructs reality in a way which is scarcely 'scientific', is in truth the only method which permits one to reproduce and intellectually grasp reality. 'Concrete totality is, therefore, the category that governs reality.'[13] The contradictions which research at first discovers in immediate reality do not have to be effaced and surmounted, but integrated as constitutive elements of a structural analysis.

Lukács then arrives at the problem of partial historical studies and the relation to the global meaning of history. We will call this, in Heideggerian language, the relation between the ontic studies of history and the ontological study of Being and its historicity. To my astonishment, I confess, it must be said that Lukács's study is not absolutely radical and, in certain ways, approaches Heideggerian dualism. I have already said that in speaking about immediately given facts, Lukács also admitted — contrary to the first of the *Theses on Feuerbach* and to the results of recent epistemological studies, notably those of Piaget — that the perception of isolated objects and facts could be validly known, that it constituted a sort of independent datum, and that integration into totality, into the whole of history, was only important in order to know their pertinence, their meaning and their function. It follows — and Piaget has convincingly demonstrated this — that, as Marx says in the first of his *Theses on Feuerbach*, even in the organization of perceptible and immediate data, the structuration of perceptive objects is closely bound to praxis, and that means to history. It seems to us this lacks the radical aspect found in the paragraph on historical knowledge.

Part 2

Lectures during the 1967-8 Academic Year

1 Reification, *Zuhandenheit* and Praxis[1]

It seems quite certain that two passages in *Sein und Zeit* refer to Lukács. In the first, Heidegger himself poses the problem of what differentiates his philosophy from others, and he distinguishes it from three others. He names Scheler and personalism; Dilthey and *Lebensphilosophie*; but in the third case, the one who — according to the author — defends himself on the ontic level against the reification of consciousness (*Verdinglichung des Bewusstseins*), he does not mention anyone by name. It is very probable, nevertheless, that in 1927 he could only have meant Lukács. Here is what Heidegger writes:

> One of the first tasks (of analysis) will be to show that to begin research by starting from the immediately given Me and the subject, is to miss the phenomenal aspect of *Dasein* (which can be interpreted by man, despite all the Heideggerian reserves which are, moreover, put forward here in the following sentences). Any idea of the subject, if it is not based upon a fundamental ontology, falls into this ontological error of the subject, no matter what the effort is to defend it on the ontic level (therefore, the scientific level) against the 'substance of the soul' and the 'reification of consciousness'. First, reification must itself be ontologically justified for one to be able to speculate about what one positively comprehends under a non-reified being of the subject, the soul, the consciousness, the person, etc.

Heidegger states that traditional ontology is an ontology of the subject and the object, and that it is in fact fundamental for his own thought, for the philosophy he is developing, to reject any opposition between the subject and the object, any

27

assertion of a subject who finds himself opposite an object. This is to reject a mode of knowledge which propounds at the outset positive data and as a counterpart, value judgments. But, with respect to Lukács and the philosophy of the reification of consciousness, he says that this thought still finds itself at the ontic level of the separation between the subject and the object, that we are still at the level of the subject. This objection, while terminologically exact, is philosophically inexact and is due to a misunderstanding which we will come back to later on.

The second text in *Sein und Zeit* which refers to the reification of consciousness presents, in relation to the first, two different characteristics which give it a particular importance. The first time, the reification of consciousness is cited together with two other philosophies; this time only the reification of consciousness is mentioned and, again, without anyone being named. The second characteristic, the more important one, is the position of this text in *Sein und Zeit*: it is found on the last page of the book, in the conclusion. *Sein und Zeit* was to have had a second volume, which never followed; despite that, although the book concludes with the problematic of the reification of consciousness, this last page has a basic importance for the whole book.

> That past ontology [Heidegger writes] worked with the concepts of things and that the danger of the reification of consciousness exists has been known for a long time. But what does reification mean? What is its origin? Why is Being understood, above all, by starting from what is there (*Vorhanden*), what is given, and not from instrumentality (*Zuhanden*), which is nevertheless nearer? Why does this reification continuously predominate? What is the positive structure of consciousness which sees to it that reification is not adequate for it? Does the distinction between consciousness and the thing suffice to pose the ontological problematic? Are the answers to these questions forthcoming? Can one even seek an answer as long as the question about the meaning of Being is not posed or clarified?

The position of this text gives particular significance to the problem of reification and indicates that it is a central problem of the discussion for Heidegger.

Is this a direct reference to Lukács? In *History and Class Consciousness* reification is the most essential concept, and the chapter devoted to it, the basis of the other texts, is the longest in the book. It is entitled 'Reification and the Consciousness of the Proletariat', clearly indicating that the problem of reification is a problem of the transformation of consciousness, of the structuration of an inadequate consciousness, and that the proletariat is the only social group able to abolish reification and to achieve a non-reified consciousness. Most likely this is a discussion between two fundamental books which, moreover, represent an analogous turning-point, while being entirely opposed to each other. Concrete research would be necessary to resolve this. Perhaps there were discussions about these problems among Lask's circle, who was oriented toward Hegelianism, and it is not impossible that the books of Lukács and Heidegger are responses to those problems. Research should also be undertaken on Simmel's attitude, although for him the concept is not central as a philosophy of reification.

It should also be noted that *'Verdinglichung des Bewusstseins'* is always between inverted commas in Heidegger's text and that, as an added irony, they are in fact quotation marks. These terms do not, therefore, refer to some idea or other expressed differently by one of the philosophers whom Heidegger frequently mentions in his book (Husserl or Bergson, among others), but to specific concepts used by a thinker who is not named. Furthermore, it would be difficult to refer reification to Marx, first, because the analysis of the reified consciousness only takes up one chapter in *Capital* and second, because Marx uses the term 'commodity fetishism'. It was in 1922 that Lukács translated 'commodity fetishism' as 'reification'.

According to Heidegger, this entire problematic of reification is valid. Yet it is situated at the level of science, pertains to the ontic, and can only be clarified by ontological investigations which are not concerned with science. For Lukács too, the problem is posed to science, but remains a philosophical one, because for him the two are inseparable. When, starting from this terminology, Heidegger considers the philosophy of the reification of consciousness as an ontology of the subject and places it on the ontic level of science and of the separation of subject and object, he fails to recognize the specificity of Lukács's procedure, who consistently uses the old phraseology and its distinctions in order to deny them and, in order to discuss the non-existence of value judgments and judgments of fact, is obliged to discuss them separately. The determination of these terms, their absolute opposition, moreover, results from the process of reification which concerns social and economic reality just as much as the consciousness of the subject.

Lukács himself had pointed out his procedural difficulties in the introduction to his book, of which the fundamental thesis is that, in order to pass from positivist knowledge to positive and philosophical knowledge, it is necessary to surmount the subject-object opposition. Also, one must start from the idea that, in society, the being who thinks of this corresponds to the world vision of a social group, and thus, in thinking about society, the social group also thinks about itself, so that there is no separation between the subject and the object.

There is a close affinity between Heidegger and Lukács in the analysis of what Heidegger calls 'traditional ontology' and Lukács calls traditional philosophy or positivist thought, and knowledge which consists in fact in the distinction between judgments of fact and value judgments, in the assertion that knowledge of objects can be had independently of the subject; in fact, then, in the assertion that there is a subject and an object. On this point Lukács and Heidegger strictly agree: the world is not there, immediately given opposite the knowing consciousness who knows it, in so far as it is, and who eventually judges it. To use the language of Piaget, the very object, the formal ascertainment of positivism — the presence here of a cigarette-lighter — is not a fact, but already a construction: every thought implies a construction of the subject. There is no given world, the object is constructed, and its inseparability with the subject even goes as far as their identity — partial, in my opinion, but total according to Lukács — in the social sciences. The Lukácsian concept of *Gegenstandsstruktur* has been translated into French as 'objectivité' — objectivity — but this concept is in opposition to any idea of absolute objectivity. Objectivity does not exist. There is only the structuration of the object by the subject.

Heidegger sees in Descartes the fundamental point where this rupture between the subject and object is determined, with the Cartesian philosophy of the knowing and thinking ego, and its insoluble problem of knowing how this ego succeeds in knowing the real, since it is first of all a knowing ego characterized by interiority. Lukács poses exactly the same problematic but, in view of the inspiration of his work, which is not aimed at philosophers, he does so at the level of the ideological problems of his time. However, another profound difference divides the two thinkers concerning the interpretation of this problematic, a difference having its basis in that which separates the two philosophies.

For Heidegger a duality exists between the two dimensions, the authentic and the inauthentic, the onto-logical and the ontic. On the one hand, the inauthentic, the ontic, the division of subject and object, the ascertainment and the position of the world as existing, given, *Vorhanden*; this position is based either on know-ledge or, as Heidegger says — and Lukács to some extent — on a kind of technical practice. Man finds himself in inauthenticity, in the world of evil, and when, at this level, without really thinking about it, he rises to the summit of culture, he does philosophy and metaphysics and produces this pseudo-ontology of the given world and of the subject who is in opposition to it. That holds for everyday consciousness and positive science, recognized, moreover, by Heidegger as valid in its domain, and this holds just as well for philosophy. It is not by recalling the other dimension, authenticity, which we shall be coming back to, that philosophy reaches the basic ontological awareness which conceives of *Dasein* in its project, as correlative to the world within which its project is found. The existence of these two dimensions in Heidegger is a sort of prime ontological fact: that is the way in which. . . . The world is described on the basis of a pre-understanding, it is a matter of a phenomenological description of what must be understood and accepted, even if — according to Heidegger —

phenomenology must first search for the meaning of Being, which is not immediately given.

For Lukács, the question is entirely different: the given is only an empirical fact in need of construction, in need of a scientific explanation asking why, how, in what situation, at what moment, in what way, and for what function. If, at a certain moment, men think thus, that does not raise a problem of phenomenological description, but rather a scientific problem. How is it that at a certain moment individuals at the level of daily consciousness, scientists engaged in the positive sciences, philosophers engaged in philosophy, find themselves in this position of the division of subject and object?

Heidegger separates science from philosophy, into which science does not penetrate. For Lukács, on the other hand, no philosophical problem is validly posed unless we have translated it into scientific terms. There is no positive science of human facts valid in itself which a philosophy, just as valid in itself, could complete. Therefore, it is at the level of scientific research that it must always be demonstrated why positivist analysis is not valid and why philosophical analysis gives us a better understanding of the problem. But it is also, inversely, when we pose the problem at the philosophical level, that it is necessary to pose it historically in order to seek a positive explanation for it. The affinities and the differences between the two philosophies which concern us appear at each level. The problem is analogous, since it is a question of going beyond the subject/object opposition and traditional ontology. The answers are different because for Heidegger science is separate from philosophy, and history is the history of a two-dimensional spirit; whereas for Lukács, science and philosophy are inseparable in the comprehension and explanation of a single history, which is not immediately given and is 'to be made' in science and praxis.

The real subject of all historical action for Lukács (inspired by Marx), the subject of all human action, is a plural subject; the subject which at the same time is an object, since it is itself that it understands, and since it acts upon a society of which it forms a part. At the essential level of decisive historical action, of philosophy and of culture, this plural subject is a privileged group, a class, which is oriented toward the global organization or re-organization of society, hence the terms history and class consciousness. With regard to the individual 'subject' — and Heidegger's *Dasein* is only an individual — it is untrue that the universe is not a given fact, that a house, the concept of a house, is not a given fact before which this subject finds itself. If it is a matter of understanding the house, social organization, law, art, the state or any cultural and historical reality as a product of the subject and in permanent transformation, they should be referred to the groups which have made them. But an individual 'subject' finds himself in the situation — which Heidegger and Lukács have both described — of this consciousness opposite a world which is there, a world in relation to which the individual can orientate himself at the technical level or which he can judge at the level of value judgments.

According to Lukács, the separation between the subject and object, between judgment of fact and value judgment, appeared in a certain precise historical condition, with the development of the Western bourgeoisie and of the generalization of market production, with the phenomenon of reification. Determined by this reification, the world is represented as a spectacle, as an object studied from the outside, with man as one of the elements of this world, a given fact in it, who can be studied at the level of positivist sociology. This reification concerns not only the world, 'the object', but extends to psychic structures which are not only considered as facts (*Vorhanden*), but, in some of their aspects, disappear and appear as the property of things. Totality as well as the collective subject are thus no longer perceived, and practical human relations no longer exist except through the price, on the market, between buyer and seller, between individuals apparently free, isolated, and equal.

The radical break between the judgment of fact and value judgment, ascertained between the individual and the world, where the world appears as given (*Vorhanden*), is an illusion, according to Lukács, which does simply come from a fundamental structure of the human being as one of his two permanent and eternal possibilities — as Heidegger believes — but which results from that other illusion, born of reification, in which is also rooted every philosophy which begins with the individual subject, with the 'I'. The market has abolished the perception of totality — the *Dasein* of Heidegger — at every level. Let us take one example from among many: that of the disappearance of Quesnay's *Tableau économique*, since Smith and for over a century. In fact, in speaking of *homo oeconomicus,* of the individual who appears on the market, or of Robinson and his needs, the totality of production disappears from consciousness, as at other levels other representations of totality, such as the community and God, disappear. There also, philosophy and thought on the 'I', that of Descartes or, to continue our example, those of Smith and Ricardo in political economy, begins.

In this connection Lukács analyses the genesis of the transcendental subject, an analysis which has no equivalent in Heidegger's work. This subject appeared at the time of the French Revolution, when it was wished to introduce into philosophy the idea of a relation between man and the world, when the old Cartesian separation was no longer acceptable. What was essential for Kant and Fichte, as for Descartes, was the individual subject bound to the atomization of the market production society. This individual empirical 'subject' — whether Tom, Dick and Harry or Immanuel Kant — finding himself always and inevitably in an already given world, could not be the basis of this relation with the world nor could he be the constitutive subject of this world. The new problematic was, then, both to refer the world to a subject without which it had no meaning, and to keep the ego as the individual subject, without introducing the collective subject bound to history and totality. It is starting from this problematic of two positions, in themselves irreconcilable, that the different forms of the transcendental subject are born: the world is constituted by the subject, but this subject is not the empirical subject of the positive sciences, it is not the subject studied by sociology and psychology, it is a sort of philosophical construction which is generally called consciousness or the transcendental subject.

34

In comparison with this philosophical construction, Lukács stresses the great superiority of the Marxist dialectic because there the subject, without which the world cannot be understood, is a plural subject: since for Marxism, although the world is the object, the subject itself is the object and the object is the subject. Any historical world at a given moment is materially and intellectually constituted by collective subjects which can only be conceived by dialectical and philosophical knowledge. The relation between the world, the significant universe in which men live, and the men who create it is inseparable, a relation in a double sense: the subject is part of the world and in fact introduces meaning there practically, but this world is part of the subject and constitutes it. This circle, a vicious circle for a static philosophy, is no problem for the dialectical study of history. In his *Theses on Feuerbach*, Marx said that conditions create men but that, in given conditions, men create new conditions and that in their praxis they transform themselves by transforming the world.

According to Lukács, then, the transcendental subject is born within individualist thought in order to resolve the problems of that thought, but without succeeding, without being able to escape from reification which is at the origin of the philosophy and the thought of the ego in all its forms. This historical, economic, and social phenomenon of reification is at the basis of the epistemological transformation described by Heidegger and Lukács, and which only the latter explains. Both wish to go beyond the antinomies of this epistemology. To traditional ontology they oppose two fundamental concepts: *Zuhandenheit* and *praxis*, and we will discover — with regard to these two concepts — the same correspondence and the same difference between their two philosophies. The essential idea of these two concepts already existed in the first of Marx's *Theses on Feuerbach:*

> The main fault of any former materialism — including that of Feuerbach — is that the object, reality, and the tangible world are only grasped in the form of an *object* or an intuition, but not as a *concrete human activity,* as an *experience* in a subjective way.

Feuerbach forgets that intuition is an activity, a perceptive activity, that there is no object separate from the subject, given in a passive and contemplative intuition, that one does not perceive a world which is given, but that this world is created under certain conditions. It is this activity which we find in the Heideggerian concept of *Zuhandenheit*, that is to say manageability, instrumentality, the concept opposed to *Vorhandenheit*, to what is there, available. *Dasein* is primarily in a world where objects are *Zuhanden*, in the hand, objects which are not independent of qualities and which are there in the light of an action oriented toward an end. Heidegger gives the example of the hammer, as hammer for pounding, which one does not see as a hammer, but which appears as such when it functions badly, because it is too heavy and can no longer be taken into one's hand, or because it breaks or because other additional tools are lacking. Then the hammer is seen as a hammer and ceases to be *Zuhanden*. It appears as being there, *Vorhanden*, as being that which can be indicated in a judgment.

In this example, Heidegger gives us a phenomenological description of the genesis of availability, a very different genesis from that which we find in Lukács with regard to theory and reification — the pathology of pure theory and the invariable — which Lukács distinguishes but which are not distinguished in Heidegger's description. For the isolated animal who is without language, consciousness or tools, for the animal who exists as an individual subject, the distinction between subject and object is meaningless, the object is inseparable from its perception in action. But the human subject is a plural subject and this world of *Vorhandenheit* — which for Heidegger appears along with the obstacle, at the moment activity is interrupted — is permanent and necessary in human praxis founded upon the division of social labour, upon work in common, which is impossible without language. Collective praxis, without which there is no hammer, presumes the possibility of passing to the level of *Vorhandenheit*, by means of discussion and language; the relation between perception and behaviour is necessarily mediated there. *Vorhandenheit*, then, is not derived from *Zuhandenheit* solely as a result of obstacles, as Heidegger believes: it constitutes a fundamental moment of it.

What appears to be an accident for Heidegger is a necessary moment in all human action. It would be asking the circular question about origins and wondering which came first, the chicken or the egg, to wonder whether it is language and the psychological possibility of symbolism which have made society possible or, on the contrary, whether it is the existence of society which has produced language. Undoubtedly, what Piaget calls *'un choc en retour'* (a rebound) has occurred, language and society have acted on each other. Moreover, society should not be conceived in the Durkheimian sense as a pre-existing entity which imposes itself upon the individuals who constitute it by producing their life together. In any case, the existence of a theoretical level is not an illusion, but an inevitable necessity.

Language is bound to every experience and there is no experience without language. One must not think, however, like the contemporary structuralists, that everything is only language upon language. This is an ideological restriction of praxis, the fact that everything is an action upon an action, but action presumes theory and language as a moment. It is the task of positive and philosophical sociology to discover, each time, the mediations between theory and experience despite fixations and oppositions, to understand theory and consciousness, however abstract it may be, in the identity of the subject and the object, on the basis of collective praxis.

Lukács and Heidegger both reject the preliminary assertion of a subject, one which would be primarily a subject of knowledge opposite a world, which would also exist only for knowledge and would be constituted by it; a given world of objects, having its existence in itself and, as a counterpart, value judgments toward the subject which would be outside.

The common origin of their criticism seems rather evident to us. There is no basic difference between the Heideggerian position and the *Theses on Feuerbach*, according to which consciousness is always bound to praxis. In his action — which begins with perceptive activity — the subject constitutes the world, and this world must be understood on the basis of its constitution at all levels, which results in transforming science into philosophy. As was already explained to us in *Sein und Zeit, Dasein* is always already in a world where objects are primarily and fundamentally *Zuhanden* and are not in the first place objects of consciousness but objects having qualities, present in the light of an action oriented toward an end. But this proximity should not cause one to forget the equally essential difference between Lukács and Heidegger. In *Sein und Zeit, Zuhandenheit* is only analysed as a psychic phenomenon of consciousness, which only appears for the latter with its suspension, after the accident, with *Vorhandenheit*. According to the dialectical thought of Lukács, on the other hand, praxis is not individual, and theory and *Vorhandenheit* are a constant part of it.

This difference between *Zuhandenheit* and *praxis* has an immediate consequence for the problem of truth. According to Heidegger, the problem of the adequation of the representation with the object is bound to the false ontology of *Vorhandenheit* of the world which is there, separated from the subject and its project. Heidegger explains that truth has a fundamentally different character, that it concerns the mode of being authentic or inauthentic. According to this Heideggerian conception the definition of truth loses all its scientific character. His answer is limited by the absence in his thinking of an effective conception of action because action only exists in *Sein und Zeit* as thought about action, as the authentic project for the great historical figures. His objection against representation is valid, and he is not the first to have formulated it against traditional philosophy. In fact, what does the coincidence between the representation and the object mean, since the object itself is only a representation? To this objection Lukács answers that truth is the possibility of orienting oneself in praxis. The scientific conception is derived from the project — as Heidegger also admits —. but a problematic on the scientific order exists all the same, which is not only that of authenticity or inauthenticity: it is a question of knowing to what extent this project is, or is not, realizable with the representation which is bound to it. But this is a problem for science which has no place in Heidegger's thought. The basis of this truth, this possible orientation in praxis, is, for Lukács, the transindividual subject which itself is the object — hence the objective character of its possibility — which science can study, whereas, if the possible also characterizes *Dasein* for Heidegger, this permanent and abstract possible is not, and could not be, objective. The opposing perspective between individual *Dasein* and the collective subject, which we discover in other concepts of Heidegger and. Lukács, also differentiates the meanings of *Zuhandenheit* and praxis.

2 Totality, Being and History[1]

The fundamental problem common to Lukács and Heidegger is that of man's inseparability from meaning and from the world, that of the subject-object identity: when man understands the world, he understands the meaning of *Dasein*, the meaning of his being and, inversely, it is in understanding his own being that he can understand the world. The two thinkers reject, as false ontology, any philosophy which presents a theory of totality or Being, based on the opposition between subject and object. These — totality and Being — are the two central and related categories which the two philosophers have introduced and which distinguish them from the Neo-Kantianism prevailing in their time as well as from Husserl's thought.

What Heidegger tells us about the category of Being had already been discovered by Lukács in relation to totality. Being is not the most general and empty category or concept. In fact it is not a concept, but a basic reality from which the *Dasein* questions. Its character is *temporal, meaningful*, and *historical*.

In *History and Class Consciousness* totality is no longer a given, not something we can speak about in the indicative, for the simple reason that we, and with us the subject, are inside it, and the object, the world constituted by the activity of the collective subject, is in the subject which derives from it. Second, this totality is significant because it is related to human activity and because men always create meaningful realities. No definition is possible in the human sciences. Their meaning is always discovered and, for that reason, they are a union of value judgments and judgments of fact. Meaning and its discovery have an eminently historical character and, for both Lukács and Heidegger, authenticity is situated in relation to history. This relation to history is, nevertheless, conceived of in a basically different way by each of the two thinkers.

Despite their differences, which are fundamental, Lukács and Heidegger both effect a critical return to the philosophy of Hegel. In his chapter on history, Heidegger explains what separates him from the latter: Hegel attempted to bring together historicity and the natural sciences in order to construct his concept of time by starting from points, therefore from space, in order to apply this concept of time − which comes from the natural sciences − to the development of the mind. Lukács, who considered the separation between the natural sciences and those of the mind necessary, also criticizes their identification. He does not, however, refer directly to Hegel, but to Engels, who defended the Hegelian position on this point. (This criticism of Engels, by the way, caused him a lot of difficulty among his Marxist friends.)

On the ontological side, the problematic of Being is situated in phenomenological research, according to Heidegger. The sciences, which ignore their own foundations and are entrenched in empirical and ontic statements, can remain as they are and stay outside research. This duality between ontology and the ontic − which is basic to Heidegger's thought − is found in his work at other levels, in the opposition between the authentic and the inauthentic, for example, or in the two-dimensional conception of history characterized by the return to the authentic and the decline into the inauthentic. This inauthenticity is a primary fact, authenticity projecting itself simply as a duty, considered as a permanent and abstract possibility which the individual *Dasein* can in each case choose.

On the other hand, Lukács connects History to collective subjects and does not confine it to the élites as does *Sein und Zeit*. In *History and Class Consciousness* particular historical phenomena, the forms, are at a certain level universal realities which the whole human community participates in. Starting

41

from this conception, one finds in Lukács a category which Heidegger finds contemptible: progress, or recession, bound to objective possibility. The field of the possible, according to Lukács, is not once and for all open to *Dasein* as it is for Heidegger: it belongs to the historical and not to the ontological order, and is constantly transformed by the action of collective subjects. In contrast, for Heidegger this category belongs to the ontic order and is beyond possibility which must be understood on the fundamentally different ontological plane. It is, moreover, in relation to this ontological possibility that one can speak about authenticity or inauthenticity.

Objective possibility can be studied with the help of what Lukács calls attributive consciousness or possible consciousness. But the latter, according to Lukács, cannot penetrate into the consciousness of collective subjects and be conceived by them, save in the particular and historically exceptional case of the proletariat. The objective character of the possibility each time permits and requires a scientific study of its field, a scientific study which in its turn is only valid if it remains open to the project and the possible. Thus, while admitting the necessity of science, Lukács opposes all positivist sociology and the procedure which reduces man to things and science to the level of photographic evidence. This very reduction, as we have already remarked, poses for Lukács a problem of a historical order which science must study. In the Lukácsian theory of reification, philosophy and science are inextricably interconnected, and the latter tries to explain how the world is represented in it — with spatial categories — as a spectacle, as a uniform object approachable from the outside.

Nevertheless, to be more precise, one must add that the Lukácsian concept of reification cannot in any way be reduced or likened to Bergson's concept of spatialization: Lukács criticizes the predominance of the invariable, but admits mediation and concepts. Yet, there have perhaps been influences, which in no way diminish the basic differences between the two. Recently, Gabel has tried to identify the spatialization of Bergson with Lukács's theory of reification, but he has met up with a delicate problem: that of science.

For Bergson all spatialization bound to action is of the order of false consciousness and, for him, science also spatializes; for Lukács on the contrary, it is the absence of praxis which produces reification (and, moreover, no spatialization ends in false consciousness, but simply in its hypertrophied form: reification). If, as Gabel believes, following Bergson, all spatialization is false consciousness, one can no longer defend science — which, nevertheless, Gabel considers to be true consciousness. Lukács criticizes reification but, in doing so, does not revert to a mystical position.

According to *History and Class Consciousness*, one must scientifically explain how men become given elements in a world of spectacle where their social relations are hidden as such and appear as the property of things outside of them. One must understand, starting from new social relations, which is the aim of totality, how mental structures are transformed, reified, atomized, and rivetted to givens. It is by starting from commodity fetishism that Lukács understands and explains the birth of this world of the spectacle and its corollary: the individual subject, who finds himself in its presence and relates to it, via an entire series of dualisms such as subject/object, infinite/finite, essence/appearance, value/fact, and today one could add ontological/ontic.

In discussing a formula attributable to the principal revisionist theoretician Bernstein — a formula which became a famous slogan at the time: 'the movement is all, the goal is nothing' — Lukács poses the problem of dualism pertaining to the relations between means and ends. Dualism is a vision of the object represented as a purely external objectivity, independent of or opposed to the subject; and we have said that for the individual it cannot be otherwise. Only two attitudes are possible for this individual subject: the technical or the ethical. All other possibilities finally lead back to it and the variations can be reduced to it. The technical attitude affirms the primacy of ends, which must be realized at all costs, and to which the means, whose importance is secondary, must be subordinated. The ethical attitude, on the contrary, subordinates the end to the means and always wishes to keep its hands clean. Only the dialectical perspective goes beyond dualism and places the subject as a

43

group, the subject as a relative totality, in relation to the world which is conceived as process and totality.

Within the oriented praxis of the transindividual subject, the object can be understood and explained. Contrary to Bernstein, Lukács maintains that, in the totality constituted by the close relation between essence and appearance, the end penetrates each given element at a given moment. The end is not separated from the means which it structures, since it is, for its part, constantly structured by them, consequently, the sole possibility of understanding an object and a social reality is not only to take into account the immediately given element, but also its structured development, its orientation toward structuration. One must integrate the influence of the process in and on the result. Thus, when one studies a phenomenon, one must make an analysis of it genetically: the structuralism of Lukács — and of those inspired by him — is a genetic structuralism. It is not the result, the structure, which is interesting independently of its history, because it is bound to its genesis which is just as structured. Inversely, history must also be studied in its structures. At the level of action and on the epistemological level, the end and the means constitute a structured unity in relation to a plural subject. The latter — as opposed to the transcendental *ego* — is not a philosophical composition and can at any moment be known. The great superiority of the transindividual subject over the transcendental *ego,* is that it is not opposed to an object, it always has an empirical character in the world, and it is traceable via research: it is men who have acted during the course of history and who are the origin of objects, works, and ideas. These are the collective subjects which can be studied. The transcendental ego — whose origin has been traced from the dualist vision of the world — tries in vain to transcend this dualism. On the other hand, it disappears the moment one discovers the inseparable relation between the significant universe in which men live, from which they come, and these same men who create it, when one discovers that this plural subject is part of the world and in fact introduces meaning into it through praxis, and that the world is also part of it and constitutes it.

Collective praxis, the foundation of the conception which

Lukács develops in *History and Class Consciousness*, does not exist for Heidegger. Despite the *Sein* as the central 'category', and despite the break with the transcendental *ego* — although *Dasein* is a type of philosophical construction — *Sein und Zeit* is still trapped in a dualism with its oppositions between the ontological and the ontic on the one hand, and between philosophy and science on the other. Contrary to Lukács who, starting from commodity fetishism and the collective subject, succeeds in explaining the genesis of the given world as a spectacle, Heidegger does not go beyond a phenomenological description of the world of evil and of inauthenticity, and has not succeeded in explaining its historical source. Traditional ontology, whose origin *Sein und Zeit* does not explain, appears — at least implicitly — to be bound to the world of *Mitsein*, to the absorption of philosophers into this inauthentic world which defines man by starting from the given and treats him as an object. In contrast, the basic ontology which Heidegger wishes to develop is based on understanding *Dasein* as that which cannot be oriented toward itself without raising the question of Being, as that which can only do so by raising the question of meaning and by being open to the project and the possible.

In Heidegger's book it was the analysis of *Dasein* which primarily attracted attention. And one essential aspect of *Sein und Zeit*, the problematic of Being (the difference between Heidegger and Sartre), was completely misunderstood initially. The public saw in this book not so much the philosophy of history, the philosophy of Being as totality, as the particular problematic, as Heidegger formulated it, of the world of authenticity and inauthenticity, that of dereliction, of fear and anguish. At first only the thought of being-toward-death was noted, and at first sight it seemed that the whole introductory chapter on *Sein* was useless, that the essential part began with the analysis of *Dasein*. This analysis inaugurated existentialism as a philosophy of limit, but Lukács had already outlined this idea of limit in one of his first texts, 'The Metaphysics of Tragedy'.

This is one of the essays which make up *The Soul and the Forms*, a work published in 1911 which, however, unites texts already published, for the most part in Hungarian or German reviews. Going back to before the nineteenth-century university philosophy, Lukács in his book links up again with the tradition of classical thought and conceives man essentially through his search for the absolute. A preliminary essay — written on the occasion of the book's publication — attempts to distil the essence of the essay. Starting from a concrete reality, the essay, according to Lukács, poses the problem of meaning without being able to produce a systematic reply to it. That reply, being the competence of philosophy, remains outside the possibilities of the essay, which can only mention it. Here, the essay is essentially an ironical form because it raises basic questions, but at random, which, however, pertain to incidents or to forms at times in themselves deprived of importance. Each essay in the book deals with a form: the forms are, for the young Lukács, significant structures — hence the title: *The Soul and the Forms* — which are artistic forms or forms of existence which manifest psychic structures whose authenticity Lukács questions. Lukács has, perhaps, sensed the affinity of this manner of questioning to Kierkegaard's ironical attitude, and he devotes one of the main essays of his book to the latter, undoubtedly one of the first texts, which from before the First World War, re-established the Danish thinker. In the chapter which he devotes to him, Lukács opposes Kierkegaard and defines the central event of his life — his engagement and break with Régine — as a gesture which claims to attain, without being able to, an authentic *form*, i.e., 'the sole path toward the absolute in life'.[2] Neither does *The Soul and the Forms* show much tolerance for Kierkegaardian anxiety. This fundamentally differentiates Lukács from subsequent existentialism which he nevertheless mentions in 'The Metaphysics of Tragedy'. This text, previously published in *Logos* and republished at the end of the volume, presents Lukács's position at that time.

Returning to the Pascalian position of the 'all or nothing', without going into detail, Lukács, in his essay on tragedy, questions the values of Western individualism, dominant since the seventeenth century. There he raises in all its acuity the problem of the relations between the individual, authenticity

and death, and he conceives of man as having two possibilities, the authentic and the inauthentic, as Heidegger was
to do later on in *Sein und Zeit*. Lukács does not of course use
the later Heideggerian terminology, but in the same sense he
opposes authentic *Das* Leben (*The* life) and inauthentic das
Leben (the *Life*). He describes the inauthentic *Life* as 'an
anarchy of chiaroscuro' where nothing 'is ever completely
realized and nothing reaches the end of its ultimate possibilities, new voices are always interfering, bringing confusion to the chorus of those already resounding'. In this
inauthentic life everything 'interpenetrates shamelessly in an
impure mixture, everything is destroyed and broken, nothing
ever blooms into real life. . . . Life is the most unreal and the
least living of all the forms of existence.' The Heideggerian
description of inauthentic existence is more complex, but its
other aspects are also to be found in Lukács, not in 1911 but
in *History and Class Consciousness* (1923), in the chapters on
reification, false consciousness, and bad faith.

According to 'The Metaphysics of Tragedy', 'authentic life
is always unreal, always impossible for empirical life', there is
no passage between everyday life and authenticity, but
revelation and miracle:

> Something lights up, appears like lightening over the banal paths . . .
> luck, the great moment, the miracle. . . . The miracle is what
> determines and is determined. It penetrates life in an unforeseeable
> way, by chance and unrelated to the rest, and relentlessly transforms
> the whole in a clear and univocal reckoning.

The occasion in itself matters little;

> too strange to each other to be hostile, they face one another: the
> revealer and the revealed, the occasion and the revelation. For what
> is revealed is strange to the occasion which has produced it, it is
> higher and comes from another world. The soul, having become
> itself, measures its entire former existence with strange eyes.

In *Life* man toils and awaits the miracle which never
happens:

> This experience (*Erlebnis*) is hidden in each of life's events like a
> menacing abyss, like a door leading to the courtroom. It is the
> relation with the idea whose occurrence is only phenomenal. . . . The
> wisdom of the tragic miracle is the wisdom of limits. The miracle is

47

always clear, but all clarity separates and indicates two directions in the world. . . . Any very elevated point is a summit and a frontier, the meeting point between death and life. The tragic life is the most exclusively earthbound of all lives. That is why its limits are always confounded by death. Real (inauthentic) life never reaches this limit and only knows death as something terrible, deprived of meaning, which abruptly cuts off its course. The mystic goes beyond this limit and for that very reason deprives death of any value for reality. For tragedy on the other hand, death — the limit in itself — constitutes an ever immanent reality. . . . The fact of living this limit constitutes the soul's awakening to consciousness, self-consciousness: it exists because it is limited, and only to the extent in which (and because) it is limited.[3]

For Lukács then, the opposition is absolute between tragic grandeur and the different forms of inauthentic consciousness which, looked at from the viewpoint of tragedy, are all equal. This grandeur resides in solitude, in the rejection of all social life with others. It resides in the rejection of history. 'The Metaphysics of Tragedy' can be ranged alongside Racine and Kant and is opposed to every historical enterprise, whether Shakespeare or Hegel. The latter acknowledged tragedy, but only as one of the forms of consciousness, and integrated the consciousness of limit into a development which transcends it, into the development of the mind and history. For Lukács in 1911, the limit deprives the individual of any importance; no project, then, is any longer valid and history is impossible. Like Pascal, moreover, he has seen the limit, and he has envisaged the grandeur of man in the rejection, without anguish, of a life in which no project could be realized because the individual finds himself at the limit and in the presence of death. Heidegger, on the contrary, introduces anguish — which the tragic position of Lukács excludes — and wishes to base the project and history on Being-for-death and the thought of limit. He wishes to attain Being-with on the basis of authenticity, which is only accessible in isolation and through solitude.

For *Sein und Zeit*, history is essential, and the meaning of Being and authenticity is only found in the historical project. Being and history, these basic Heideggerian 'categories', do not exist in 'The Metaphysics of Tragedy', since for Lukács the consciousness of limit forms the basis for the choice between authenticity and inauthenticity. Totality and history appear in *History and Class Consciousness* because with the collective subject history becomes possible, the consciousness of limit disappears and death loses its importance.

Heidegger criticizes all consciousness which, living authentically, does not give death central importance and does not consider it to be the basic problem. In 1927 he effected a synthesis between two perspectives, a synthesis which Lukács always refused to make, and united a philosophy of history with a Kierkegaardian philosophy of anxiety and solitude. Heidegger does not create a philosophy of immediate experience. It is not a matter of the temporality of experience for him, but of temporality whose authentic form is historicity. It is a phenomenological philosophy which he develops, while explaining, in his chapter on phenomenology, that it is precisely the latter which must be oriented toward the meaning of Being which is not a given phenomenon. One has access to the meaning of Being not in immediate experience which is inauthentic, but historically according to authentic temporality. For *Sein und Zeit*, history, in so far as it is authentic — not the historicity of universal history, that of the immediate Being-with — is the history of individuals who become authentic in isolation and by means of a decision, before subsiding again into the inauthentic. History is made each time on the basis of a resolution whose authenticity comes from being-free-for-death and from the bond which this resolute-decision — to use the words of Heidegger — creates between the individual and the community (*Gemeinschaft*) of a people (*Volk*) through a hero from the past whom this individual has chosen, in this decision, to repeat by orienting himself toward the future. Heidegger calls this authentic being-with in the community of a People: *destiny*. It is not a matter of the human community, nor of universal history (which, according to Heidegger, is at the same level as gossip), but of the community of a people and of the authentic repetition of its former heroes. For Lukács in 1923 however, the subjects of history are groups, collective subjects who are at the same time objects. *Dasein*, that particular form of Being starting from which action and understanding are possible, is not, according to Lukács, the individual but plural subjects whose possibilities are objective.

Both for Lukács and Heidegger, meaning reveals itself in its relation to *Dasein* or in relation to the collective subject. But, determined by the individuality of *Dasein* or by the collectivity of the subject, this relation to meaning is different for the two thinkers. For Heidegger this relation is not mediated and, contrary to the authentic decision, he situates mediations in the order of universal history and through them characterizes the various forms of historicism. For Lukács, on the other hand, the passage between the event and totality, the discovery of concrete and immanent meaning, is not immediate in anything, the decision does not reveal meaning and does not give access to it. One does not leap from the positive and immediate science of the given toward the totality of Being. The problem of totality in *History and Class Consciousness* is one of concrete and progressive totalities, the goal of research being to discover their connections and their mediations. Without these mediations one ends up, according to Lukács, with a two-dimensional history, with the two corresponding bourgeois conceptions of history. First, there is the formalist attitude, an external classification plastered over historical development, like the general theory and the law of the three stages of Auguste Comte, applicable to all cases, without any regard to immanent structures and particular mediations. Second, and as a counterpart to this formalism which does not take into account the particular and concrete event, there are the irrationalist theories, with their methods founded upon intuition and empathy, which places in the forefront the role of the great personality and the élites, and insist upon the singular and imperceptible character of events and individualities, which one must understand — according to these theories — in their uniqueness, independently of any insertion in a rational development having its own laws. Contrary to these univocal and complementary conceptions, Lukács upholds the validity of dialectical analysis, whose specificity resides in the possibility of abandoning both the abstract character of the general theory and the irrational

character of the individual fact, and of rationally understanding the individual — while safeguarding the individual's
relative liberty — by starting from the field of the possible of
the plural subject and from its function in the praxis of the
group bound to the praxis of other social groups: it is by
understanding themselves in their action on the basis of this
perspective, in the awareness of the collective subject (in
other words, in de-reification), that men can have access to
human authenticity and community. It is only thus that the
conception of two-dimensional history can be transcended,
the history of formalist historicism and that of creative
individuals. This two-dimensional history is found again in
Heidegger who, starting from individual *Dasein*, recognizes no
other authenticity but the individual in isolation and in the
life for death.

As we have already pointed out: the thoughts of Lukács
and Heidegger — of the early Lukács (1909—23) and of the
early Heidegger (1927) — are homologous and related, with
basic differences of orientation which return at the level of
each problem. Their viewpoints are different and should
never be confused. In spite of which, it is difficult to imagine
their two philosophies as unrelated and on the subject of
those relations at least a Lukácsian influence should be
mentioned through the reviews and even, in a specific social
milieu, of indirect relations through Lask.

3 Objective Possibility and Possible Consciousness[1]

Every work, every action, every human situation must be understood starting from its genesis, and its genesis presupposes not only a single collective subject, but a confrontation of collective subjects. Actions have results which rarely correspond to the precise aspirations of any of these groups. An event, in fact, objectively results from an aggregate of projects and tendencies which confront each other. The subject in question here is not a consciousness present to itself, it is not a consciousness consciously aiming at a precise goal. What a subject wishes, what the action of a group tends toward, hardly ever corresponds to its consciousness, with the exception of the proletariat, according to Lukács, as we shall see later on. Even independently of this difference between the real consciousness and the projected goal, the result of a group's action also depends upon the action of other groups opposed to it and capable of thwarting it.

Every group does not understand the result — the totality — and, consequently, every group understands itself and its situation, the goals and the action of the other groups, only up to a certain point, from a viewpoint determined by its objective situation. It can be — and very often this is the case — that no group can have a consciousness vast enough to achieve this totality. Writing from the orthodox Marxist viewpoint, Lukács believed — and this is the subject of the chapter of his book on class consciousness which we are concerned with — that the proletariat, by its privileged situation, could achieve a transparent consciousness and find itself at a moment of history in which it was on the verge of doing so. But, most often, false consciousnesses, ideological consciousnesses, which are inadequate, correspond to the real tendencies of the structuration of groups.

Nevertheless, these differences between the goal and reality, these oppositions between action and conditions, should not be understood as heterogeneous oppositions conceived according to the Sartrian concept of the 'practico-inert' developed in *Critique de la raison dialectique*. For Sartre the content of this concept, contrary to action, is non-meaningful and non-dialectical. This opposition between the dialectical and the practico-inert resumes the traditional opposition between subject and object, because in fact, for Sartre the subject is an individual subject: the collective subject, the foundation of the subject-object identity, is lacking in his perspective, and collective action always appears for Sartre as a sum of individual actions organized by means of a third party. As the result of action rarely corresponds to the goals of the subjects, this result — especially when it arises from the previous action of other subjects — appears in Sartre's view as a restricting presence deprived of human meaning, like the practico-inert. It is true that man's liberty is limited, but not only by external conditions as Sartre believes: men are limited just as much by their mental structures which result from those conditions and are to be found in them. Nevertheless, these conditions and mental structures do not merely place limits on men; they also create for them a field of possibilities within which they act and modify reality while modifying themselves. Thus, they change their field of the possible. We all know Marx's famous idea that by changing nature, men change themselves and their social reality, thus creating possibilities which can be vaster and make men freer; or on the contrary, can narrow their scope in a reactionary manner. It is essential to understand that conditions are also the result of action and that every human phenomenon can be broken down into significant structures. Although they are different, subject and object are identical. The conditions, produced by other activities, are dialectical and significant on the same grounds as the action of the subject: they constitute the subject and its mental structure and are not external to it. Therefore, it cannot be said — to use a Sartrian example — that the desire for enrichment of every Spaniard, following the discovery of America, was dialectical while the result — general impoverishment — was the practico-inert.

Dialectics is the insertion of all aspects of the problem into a significant totality, such as, for example, the link which Marx established between the development of the forces of production and the impoverishment of the working classes at a given moment in historical development, or — to use yet another example from *Capital* — the interdependence between production and the market, between the rationality of production and the 'irrationality' of consumption; however, during his time the classical economy, which was concerned with a non-rationalized economic totality (as Marx was also), did not understand this interdependence of elements in its totality and separated production and the market.

Objective possibility is not simply an immanent criterion of the external situation of the group, or the individual, which acts. Objective possibility depends upon two factors which are not mutually independent, two aspects which are not even complementary but, to a certain extent, identical. On the one hand, the external situation of the group and of individuals determines them and makes certain things impossible; but, on the other hand, the mental structure of the group determines its action and acts in such a manner that certain things, certain projects, are not thinkable. Consequently, the group cannot want them, not only at the level of consciousness, but also at the non-conscious level which is essential for action. This element of mental structuration is just as important for characterizing an objective possibility as the external situation is. This mental structuration is to a very large extent determined by the external situation and the latter, in its turn, being merely the aggregate of the social relations of the group, comes from the mental structures: it is what Hegel had already termed the identity of the subject and the object.

One of the false dualities of the mechanist position consists precisely in completely separating the field of the possible created from without and the field of the possible created from within, in only seeing one or the other, or in seeing both as two different and complementary aspects which have no identical features. For Lukács, on the contrary, possible consciousness and objective possibility are inextricably linked.

In his chapter on class consciousness, Lukács studies four types of relations between possible consciousness and objective possibility. An aggregate of types of consciousnesses in pre-capitalist societies, and three interconnected categories of consciousness in the capitalist method of production. For Lukács, in contrast to Heidegger and popular Marxism, there is in general no structure of 'inauthentic' or ideological consciousness. The falseness or truth of consciousness, its ideological or non-ideological character, are determined by its relation to production returns, by its possibility of access and its proximity to the totality of social life.

First of all, Lukács broaches the aggregate of types of consciousness in pre-capitalist societies where the relations of production, although entirely fundamental, were not unified, and in which certain groups, although determined by the relations of production, were not immediately engaged in production. Lukács cites the example given by Marx of states in Asian societies where the commune, the agrarian basis of society, always remained the same and was always reconstructed, whereas the state structure could change, could be modified, and invasions could take place to demolish the former empire. The latter evidently does not mean that the groups external to the commune – the state organization – do not have an economic character, but they only directly intervene in the economy to levy various taxes there, whereas for example, the capitalist fills a precise economic function within market production. In these pre-capitalist societies, the conceptions of the world in which religious or political ideology forms the centre or the essential element of the representation of society are not as distorting as they were to be later on in the capitalist method of production. Indeed, to the extent in which, within these forms of society, the participation in the methods of production, for certain groups, is necessarily effected by means of political or religious mediations, just as in other so-called primitive societies, it is effected by means of kinship structures. Thus, according to *History and Class Consciousness*, the ideological element of these different types of consciousness would consist in misunderstanding the economic relation, that is to say, in misunderstanding the relations of production. Lukács, however, recalls, according to Marx, that economic relations had a greater transparency in these societies.

Lukács briefly discusses these societies and dedicates the main part of his analysis to the various structures of class consciousness in capitalist society. To be more precise, one must add today: in liberal capitalist society. He distinguishes three types of class consciousness: that of the intermediate classes, that of the bourgeoisie, and that of the proletariat, as he conceived them from his orthodox Marxist viewpoint. He makes a basic distinction between the nature and function of these three types of class consciousness, a distinction which is, in his view, of radical importance for the praxis of the proletariat.

The analysis of the class consciousness of the *petite-bourgeoisie* continues and develops the traditional Marxist analyses which became more widespread and familiar with the rise of fascism. According to *History and Class Consciousness,* the *petite-bourgeoisie*, owing to its situation, is absolutely incapable of seeing the whole of the social structure, and cannot even orient itself toward the whole of this global structuration, precisely because it is a relic of former times which the development of capitalism and the restructuring of society tend to eliminate. It must, then, remain at the level of the immediate and relate itself to it in an affective and immediate way in order to separate the good and the bad side in society. Lukács then takes up Marx's polemic against Proudhon, in which Marx accused the ideological representative of the *petite-bourgeoisie* of trying to distinguish what is good and what is bad in capitalism, without being able to understand that the good and the bad side are only two aspects of the same functionality and a common global structuration which cannot be separated nor exist independently from each other.

In its inclination to a maximum possible consciousness — which in this case is not identifiable with its real consciousness — the *petite-bourgeoisie,* which is incapable of an overall view or of rational conceptualization, orients itself toward valuations essentially of the affective order, between what is good and what is bad in the praxis of the two other main classes of capitalist society. The *petite-bourgeoisie* oscillates between them and ends by joining up with the class which occupies the strongest position.

One could cite as an example of this attitude of the intermediate classes the case of Ilya Ehrenburg and Erich Kästner, two writers famous in their time, who in the years 1928—30 presented the world from this viewpoint as incomprehensible, paradoxical, and full of contradictions. Ilya Ehrenburg, who was essentially a novelist, was amazed and saddened by the development of technology. The German poet Kästner, turning his back on this paradoxical world, took refuge in a dream world and wrote stories for children with great skill and success. Both underwent an emotional reaction of admiration, seduction and rejection. Ehrenburg criticized Stalinism. Kästner's criticism of national-socialism was most vehement and radical. Later on, however, they suffered an unexpected, but sociologically understandable, development and their criticism ceased. The German middle classes rallied behind Hitlerism despite isolated resistance. And although things had changed, what remained of the middle classes in Russia rallied behind Stalinism. What these two writers produced is so clear that it can almost be called a mechanistic determination. Kästner did not become a fascist, nor Ehrenburg a Stalinist, but the latter suddenly returned to Russia and Kästner began to publish gothic novels in which there was none of his previous problematic. After the war they both resumed their former critical attitudes, but what is interesting in their case is that they show both an affective reaction to crisis and a rallying to it.

In the paradoxical consciousness of the *petite-bourgeoisie* which, we have just seen, cannot direct itself toward totality and achieve a rational attitude, Lukács differentiates the structuration of the consciousness of the two other classes of liberal capitalist society: the bourgeoisie and the proletariat who, as basic classes, are decisive and can, therefore, orient themselves toward a global understanding of society.

In describing the bourgeois consciousness, of which an entire series of elements can be found in Heidegger's descriptions, Lukács emphasizes one of its essential characteristics which distinguishes it from all previous class consciousnesses. The Lukácsian analysis is still situated at the level of traditional Marxist analysis and sees in the praxis of the bourgeoisie both an orientation toward the global society and the impossibility of achieving it. According to *History and Class Consciousness,* that is determined by the fact that the bourgeoisie wishes to avoid transformations, while a global understanding of society implies the idea of transcendence and change. Likewise, the bourgeoisie must also deny the class struggle, whereas an understanding of global society reveals it.

This characterization of the bourgeois consciousness has in part proved false because of Lukács's mistaken viewpoints (a mistake we will return to when dealing with the possible consciousness of the proletariat). In fact, Lukács affirmed that the bourgeois consciousness could not comprehend crises because such a comprehension would imply the discovery of the historical and transitory character of the capitalist method of production and the recognition of the limits of the bourgeoisie by itself, and would therefore signify its own historical condemnation. But bourgeois society, far from disappearing as Lukács believed, has surmounted the crises and transformed itself into a technocratic society of organized capitalism which has assured a considerable development of the forces of production. This is in part due to the fact that theorists of the bourgeoisie and its official thinkers have integrated, already at the level of economic thought, the whole of the economy — in part, in our opinion, without establishing a relation between cause and effect.

Today, the problem of economic analysis, of a model of growth and the accounts of the nation, which made economists shrug their shoulders forty years ago, has come to occupy the opening chapter of any manual of economics. The 1929—30 crisis and the existence of a planned Russian economy which resisted the crisis have been of great importance for the development of economic theory and for the solutions found. Lukács thought that crises constituted the main hazard of bourgeois praxis and thought. He believed the bourgeoisie was incapable of understanding them and, consequently, incapable of mastering them. It was found, however, that the bourgeois economy developed a complete theory of crises and that, to the extent in which the latter were able to be analysed, they no longer took on the same magnitude as before. This whole Lukácsian analysis should then be taken up again, with its limitations, and re-thought by means of a concrete analysis of the real evolution of Western industrial societies. Even the epistemological problems should be recast. For example, the essential relation which Lukács established between global vision and historical evolution is a very important problem and for the most part true. According to Lukács, totality and evolution are connected. Nevertheless, an overall view exists today which denies evolution: in fact, contemporary rationalism, born of this new orientation, is structuralist and 'structure' is, despite everything, a category of 'totality'.

It is in particular the Lukácsian conception of the consciousness of the proletariat which is the problem now. According to Lukács, the proletariat, like the bourgeoisie, is oriented in its praxis toward a global structuration and a global comprehension of society, but unlike the bourgeoisie, the proletariat does not run up against the same limitations. The proletariat does not disregard the class struggle: on the contrary, it affirms it and integrates both the future and transformation in its current praxis. Thus, the proletariat is the only class in history able to reach truth and history because it is in its own interest to want its own abolition. Whereas bourgeois consciousness runs up against limits and becomes paradoxical, because it seeks both extreme progress and the maintenance of the status quo, the proletariat can understand reality because it is oriented toward revolutionary action capable of provoking the transformation of society. The specificity of the class consciousness of the proletariat comes from the fact that it is the first social class in history to embody its own abolition in its aspirations and interests.

If, to obtain a picture of the Lukácsian analysis, we envisage the relation of possible consciousness to the interests of groups, this relation proves different for each of them. The structuration of classes in pre-capitalist societies is obviously oriented toward interests, but the latter are not directly situated in the economy, since participation in production is effected through the apparatus of the state or via organizations and religious ideologies, that is to say, through superstructures and by means of the mental categories which correspond to them. In the capitalist method of production, which more and more unifies the whole of society and integrates it into the market economy, all interest is directly oriented toward the economy and consequently, within this society mediations are no longer of a superstructural order. It has been seen that the intermediate classes could not clearly formulate their interests because they do not act as a group and cannot direct themselves toward totality: with a paradoxical world vision, they are torn between the two main classes of capitalist society. These two, the bourgeoisie and the proletariat, who are directly oriented toward the economic, know the character of the other domains to be simply that of superstructural mediation. But while the bourgeoisie looks to its own conservation as a class and, therefore, remains deprived of possibility and incapable of understanding evolution and totality, the proletariat, which is oriented toward its own abolition as a class, has the privilege, the possibility, and the power of access to truth and history. The privileged character of the proletariat in Lukács's thought should be insisted on, and the origin of its possibility: the unique specificity and particularity of the class consciousness of the proletariat comes from the fact that it is the only class in history not to desire its own affirmation and conservation.

For the other social groups in pre-capitalist societies or even within capitalist society, the structuration of class consciousness is effected on the basis of this conservation and this affirmation for the survival of the group, even if never able to achieve it, even if ending up in a tragic or paradoxical vision. On the contrary, for the proletariat it is essential for it to look to its own abolition as proletariat. Hence the particular and unique character of the proletarian revolution which is primarily a political revolution, while the bourgeoisie, for example, had already won economic power before effecting a political revolution. This tendency to the self-abolition of a class and this primarily political revolution imply another specific element of proletarian class consciousness. The political revolution of the proletariat could not succeed, on the part of that class, without a non-ideological awareness of the totality, without a perfectly true awareness — impossible for any other class in history — of the specificity of the proletariat in itself, and of the knowledge of its historical goals.

In this particular nature of the proletariat, Lukács has taken up one of the basic ideas of Marx, an idea which Marx never developed to its extreme limits but which found clear expression later in Rosa Luxemburg's work. According to this idea the proletariat, whose goal is to attain a classless society (and therefore without a proletariat), has a possible structuration of class and of consciousness essentially different from other structurations of class and consciousness, and this difference comes from the very specificity of this exceptional perspective of the proletariat, a perspective which, in its turn, this structuration must make possible. Nevertheless, if one studies historical and social development, it becomes obvious that this revolutionary consciousness never developed in the industrially advanced countries of the West. It likewise emerges that revolutions of a socialist character which have occurred in countries which are not very industrialized were realized, undoubtedly, through the proletariat, but above all with a very strong participation of the peasantry, the middle classes, and the intelligentsia. One is forced to admit that none of these groups has even envisaged or led an action tending toward its abolition as a social class.

It is, therefore, possible that this conception of the revolutionary proletariat is the weakest part of the Lukácsian analysis, and that the proletariat is not an exception to this law which requires that each group seek its own survival and predominance in society, not only at the level of its real consciousness, but also and above all at the level of this 'consciousness' which is essential for praxis and for its understanding, a non-conscious consciousness, one might say, the mental structure Lukács calls *zugerechnetes Bewusstsein* (which can be translated as attributive consciousness or maximum possible consciousness). The *zugerechnetes Bewusstsein* is determined by objective possibility, which constitutes this possible consciousness while being constituted by it.

The Marxist scheme of revolutionary development, especially in *The German Ideology,* conceives this development as the result of a reduction of capitalist society into the two main classes of society, the bourgeoisie and the proletariat, as a consequence of capitalist development, and extreme pauperization which involves the proletarization of all intermediate classes as well as the peasantry. Now, it is precisely in those societies in which the proletariat has become not the majority in society, but the most powerful group, that it has also become integrated, with very marked reformist tendencies. These tendencies cannot be explained simply by the existence of reformist parties, because the proletariat is not passive and does not constitute an object of activity for the parties. A different evolution of the proletariat would surely have eliminated reformist parties. In other countries outside the industrialized West, where the proletariat participated in the revolution as an active component, it was oriented toward its own affirmation, like the peasantry or the national groups of the middle classes.

The abolition of the proletariat by its own hand is different, according to *History and Class Consciousness,* from the abolition of the other classes. Historical evolution, in fact, always ends up with the development of the forces of production, the elimination of the class at the origin of the social transformation, and one can hope the elimination of classes and progress toward a classless society. In history all historical events are produced by the interconnected and opposed actions of several classes, of several collective subjects, which have always had ideological consciousnesses and were unable to know the truth. But the Marxist conception of the proletariat and its consciousness claims an exception: the tendency toward the abolition of classes and the proletariat as a class and, consequently, the possibility — necessary for the outcome of revolutionary action — of a true and transparent consciousness of totality and history. As we have already emphasized, in the case of the proletariat it is not a matter of this abolition which historical development always produces, but an action which has this abolition as a conscious and scientifically founded perspective.

This conception, which makes an exception of the proletariat, is the most problematic element — that is the least one can say about it today — of *History and Class Consciousness.* Yet it is the fundamental idea of the book, present on every page, which can only with difficulty be separated from the rest. It is, however, an erroneous idea, contestable for many and repudiated by Lukács himself, a repudiation which has its own basis, independently of his shrewdness *vis-à-vis* the Stalinist authorities and external restraints. At the time of the publication of *History and Class Consciousness,* Lukács thought he had arrived at a supremely privileged moment of history, on the eve of the socialist revolution in Western Europe. According to the book, in fact, mediations are reduced and the proximity between theory and praxis is exceptionally strong. For this proximity to become transparent reality and for the revolution to be realized, only the adequate awareness of the proletariat is lacking, which is in process of coming about, and *History and Class Consciousness* were to help at its birth.

Nevertheless, in Lukács's book there are other analyses on less privileged periods of history, and these analyses are equally valid for the period which Lukács thought exceptional. Lukács explained his political position in the two chapters of the book dedicated to Rosa Luxemburg: 'The Marxism of Rosa Luxemburg' and 'Critical Observations on Rosa Luxemburg's "Critique of the Russian Revolution" '. Without any exaggeration, we feel that one can call Lukács a descendant of Luxemburg, who played an important role in the history of Marxism. Rosa Luxemburg was its political and economic theorist, Trotsky its political representative, and Lukács and Korsch its philosophical expression.

63

Rosa Luxemburg, the author of *Introduction to Political Economy* and *The Accumulation of Capital* among others, was above all the great theorist of the revolutionary proletariat. Neither did Marx, still less Lenin, ever place the concept of the revolutionary proletariat at the centre of their theories in so radical a manner. According to Rosa Luxemburg, the other classes do not want revolution and only ally themselves with the proletariat in the absence of the final crisis. They will oppose it as soon as this crisis breaks out. No other class can truly attain revolutionary consciousness, whereas the proletariat, which is essentially revolutionary, tends toward this awareness spontaneously. The revolution can only result from this spontaneous revolutionary awareness: undoubtedly, this awareness is furthered by the action of militants, organizations and parties, but these militants and these organizations are themselves only the expression of the spontaneous evolution of the proletariat. In short, it is this evolution and spontaneous awareness of the proletariat which will oppose it to all the other social groups and will produce the conflict which will end up in its seizing power.

Reality has not confirmed this prognosis of Rosa Luxemburg's. No proletarian revolution has occurred anywhere, no section of the proletariat has spontaneously oriented itself toward conflict with all the other social groups which it should have wanted to eliminate from power in order to create a classless society in which it itself would disappear, and no section of the proletariat's evolution has been spontaneously revolutionary. The question should now be raised of the theoretical bases which might account for this historical evolution.

Lenin had already turned to the notion of the aristocracy of the workers in order to explain integration and reformism. These theses of Lenin — developed in *What Is To Be Done?* — are well-known, and they are in exact opposition to those of Rosa Luxemburg. According to Lenin, the proletariat spontaneously orients itself toward economism and reformism and can only achieve a revolutionary consciousness if the intellectuals introduce such a consciousness into it from outside. As we know, Lenin tempered these initial ideas, especially with the October Revolution, but in practice he was always inspired by this conception of the non-spontaneously revolutionary proletariat, a conception which finally revealed itself to be more accurate than Rosa Luxemburg's. These Leninist theses were, moreover, shared by his political adversaries, by those called at the time revisionists: especially Bernstein, but also Kautsky. The book by the social-democrat Hilferding, *Das Finanz Kapital,* has been essential for Leninist analyses of imperialism, and Bolshevik theorists have always had great admiration for the writings of Kautsky. Evidently, the conclusions of Lenin and Bernstein were anything but identical. They diametrically opposed each other. German social democracy oriented itself more and more toward integration and reformism, while Lenin organized the Bolshevik party, which was finally more important than the proletariat, in order to introduce revolutionary ideas into it and to direct the Revolution. Likewise, Lenin did not hesitate to seek and to practise an alliance with other social groups, for example with the peasantry, by promising it the distribution of land or, with the nationalist middle classes, by recognizing the right of the people to self-determination.

These concessions provoked criticism from Rosa Luxemburg. First, against German social-democracy and the Bolsheviks, she found fault with the bureaucracy and the 'bureaucratization' of the proletariat, the Party and the revolution since on the contrary, in her view, it is the revolutionary proletariat which should control the Party, the intellectuals and the militants. Next, against Lenin, she maintained that nationalism is basically reactionary and that, consequently, it is reactionary to admit, up to complete secession, the right to self-determination of the Russian people. Lenin thought that the possible consciousness of the Russian peasantry at the time could not go beyond the private appropriation of the land: he promised them therefore the dividing up of the great estates in order to win the Revolution. Rosa Luxemburg vigorously opposed this because she believed in the need to socialize the land: she demanded the immediate constitution of great agricultural enterprises. Her criticisms were determined by the essential distinction between the proletariat — according to her, the only radically revolutionary class — and the other classes opposed to capitalism. In short, she thought that, at the crucial moment, the nationalist middle classes, the *petite-bourgeoisie,* and the peasants attached to the *status quo,* despite their discontent, would be found in the camp of the enemies of the proletariat and the revolution.

Lukács and Korsch, as we have already emphasized, represented this Luxemburgian tendency in philosophical thought. Nevertheless, after 1917 and the failure of the Spartacus league in Germany, Lukács had to modify the Luxemburgian position and his own radicalism by conceding to Lenin's ideas. Thus, by continuing to insist upon the importance of spontaneity, Lukács underlines the dangers which too great an emphasis on the Party represents and rejects the transformation of the proletariat into a sort of auxiliary group. Yet, at the level of basic options, Lukács's book remains essentially Luxemburgian, and he constantly refers to her economic writings, and even partly to her political writings, and points out their analytical correctness.

These Luxemburgian conceptions and the historical situation at the beginning of the twenties made the existence of *History and Class Consciousness* possible, but these conceptions and this situation equally orient the book in this erroneous perspective, which is in evidence on every page and which must be removed if the essential methodological kernel of the book is still to be utilized. This methodological aspect of Lukács's thought has partly penetrated the universities via Mannheim and the School of Frankfurt and remains even today the essential contribution of *History and Class Consciousness.* It is independent of its political viewpoint — only significant for the history of the workers' movement, but of little interest for the history of philosophy — that Lukács's book remains an event and that it represents, like *The Soul and the Forms* and *Theory of the Novel* (but at a level fundamental in a different way), a turning-point of Western thought at the beginning of the twentieth century.

4 Subject-object and Function[1]

The use of the concepts of subject and object in *History and Class Consciousness* does not imply that Lukács supports their traditional opposition. As we have already pointed out concerning the reasons why he continues to use these concepts, as well as concerning their distinct conception, relative to tradition, he has explained at length in his introduction that it is a matter of the relations between the subject and the object. Lukács does not abolish the existence of the subject and the object, but neither does he separate them in order to oppose them in a rigid distinction. On the contrary, on every occasion he reasserts their identity. But the use of these concepts is always interpreted by other thinkers as if it were a matter of falling back into the traditional positions of philosophy and ontology. This is the basis of Heidegger's objections to Lukács, which we have already discussed above. This is also the root of the objections of Jacques Derrida, a new thinker who continues Heidegger's thought on more than one point and situates Marxism in metaphysics because, he believes, the concept of production is based on the traditional conceptions of the subject and the object.

Whereas structuralists have eliminated evolution, praxis, and the subject, Derrida tries to consider evolution and, in some manner, praxis. To do so, he has produced a new concept, '*la Différance*', which he has derived from 'différer' (to differ) and which he interprets — among other things -- in the meaning of: to go by a roundabout route in order ultimately to obtain a success. This *Différance*, according to

Derrida — who continues the Heideggerian opposition between the ontological and the ontic — is ontologically more basic than the difference (*la différence*) which derives from it. The latter — difference, according to the standard use of the term — is at the basis of philosophy and all theory in general which, being related to that which is present, is always aware of differences. In this Derrida takes up the Heideggerian idea of *Vorhandenheit*, which is derived from the more original *Zuhandenheit*; an idea which is met with in a different way in *Theses on Feuerbach* as well as in Lukács, but without this opposition which Heidegger and Derrida introduce. On the other hand, Lukács emphasizes the historical phenomena of commodity fetishism and reification and the determination of consciousness and the object by these phenomena. Lukács also admits that theory is related to differences and to the given, but he demonstrates that what constitutes a moment in all human praxis manages to become rigid and to predominate in capitalist society with the elimination of praxis and the generalization of reification.

As for *Différance*, this is for Derrida a manner of writing: it produces traces, which are changed or obliterated. Now, praxis also writes in the world, leaves traces: the spectacles one uses are traces in the world, the French and Russian Revolutions are others. It is equally true that the traces disappear and that later transformations both preserve and obliterate the old traces by creating a new world for us. Up to a certain point, Derrida's positions are very close to the Lukácsian positions, and we can in part admit them; nevertheless, his attempt entirely to eliminate any subject from history is totally opposed to the thought of Lukács. By eliminating the subject, Derrida is, from the perspective of dialectical thought, just as unilateral as the old idealism was — from Descartes to Neo-Kantianism — with its opposition of the subject and the object and its univocal conception which had the subject predominate (identified with self-consciousness) at the expense of the object, which it more or less eliminates.

For Lukács, it is not a matter of denying the object or the subject, but of denying their opposition. Every social phenomenon is always one of interconnected praxis, consciousness, action and thought. The subject of this praxis is a collective subject, which acts in relation to the action of other collective subjects; and this subject is a part of society, the object of its action, society itself being a part of the subject whose mental categories · it constitutes. These categories effect its thought and action, so that the subject is in the object, the object in the subject and they can neither be separated nor, with greater reason, opposed. This identity of the subject and the object, as well as the category of totality, constitutes the essence of Marx's thought for Lukács, even independently of the validity or the non-validity of all the particular and empirical analyses of Marx. According to Lukács, Marxism is above all a method which permits one to tackle social facts, to comprehend them and to decide on the attitude to adopt toward them.

The first problem presented to us, if we wish to use the Lukácsian method for the comprehension and explanation of actions and works, is that of the object. What is an object in research?

Objects such as scandal, democracy, revolution or dictator-ship do not exist because they are generalities and do not have significant structures. Positive sociology will always be able to allege that it is an eternal problem of research to remain either at the empirical level without rising to the level of law or, on the contrary, at the level of generalities; but that, despite this, it is always possible to start from the general law and then progressively approach the individual. A gradation of this kind, going from extreme generality − for example types of scandal or types of dictatorship − to such and such an individual dictatorship or one particular scandal, we repeat, just simply does not exist. Research based on the individual or the general are, and will remain, non-operative and insufficient. Nor is it a matter of starting from two poles and seeking a middle way, but of immediately directing oneself toward a signficative structure. For example: the post-revolutionary Bonapartist dictatorship, which could include, for example, Stalin, the second Cromwell, Napoleon, etc., dictatorships which have common sociological charac-teristics. The significant structure of these forms of dictator-ship − which Marxist literature has elaborated and defined −

is not that of a stage between the general and imaginary theory of all dictatorships — ranging from Caesar to the petty Latin American dictator by way of Hitler — and the case of a particular dictatorship which the historian is studying. As we have already emphasized, Lukács criticizes at length this conception of history which oscillates between the formalism of the general law and the irrational nature of the individual case. The criterion for the validity of research is the possibility of overcoming this paradox, the possibility of constituting the object in a significant structure, in other words, the possibility of discovering its function in the praxis of collective subjects.

The given object, the fact which is given and must be ascertained, is a preconception of positivism. Objects only exist as correlative to a subject and in relation to this subject's praxis. Referring to the analyses of Marx, Lukács uses the example of the discovery of variable capital in its difference with constant capital — that is to say, the difference in the capitalist method of production between wages and the rest of the capital of the enterprise — whereas in the classical economy only fixed and circulating capital were known. The classical economy, which based its theories on the viewpoint of the individual capitalist, only distinguished circulating capital, which renews itself in each production cycle, and opposed it to fixed capital — the workshop, machinery, etc. — which requires a certain number of production cycles in order to be written off. Thus, for bourgeois economics, wages and raw materials were included in the same category of circulating capital. From the capitalist point of view, the difference between raw materials and wages could not be noted, and in any case apparently had no meaning. This distinction poses the problem of the origin of surplus value, knowledge of which is fundamental for the proletariat. It raises the question of the transcendence and transformation of capitalism, all questions which, from the viewpoint of the bourgeois economist must be eluded and eliminated. But when Marx approached capitalism from the historical point of view, as a specific stage of production characterizing a certain historically determined epoch of human history, he made this distinction between wages and raw materials, and later on, between variable and constant capital, which he always considered as one of his greatest discoveries. He found a difference within what for bourgeois economics constituted an identity, and was thus able to study the different function of wages, its fundamental role in the theory of surplus value and for the understanding of the market with regard to the possibilities of sales and consumption, possibilities developed in the famous equations which Rosa Luxemburg was to take up later on in *The Accumulation of Capital.* By changing his viewpoint, Marx introduced a new object, without in any way denying the old distinction between fixed and circulating capital, which also has its function and which he studied in detail. The truth does not consist in rejecting one of the two distinctions as false, but in studying its function and in understanding that, in a certain perspective, also determined by the function of the object, the latter is different in relation to the other perspectives and according to other functionalities. This is what must be understood by *Gegenstandsstruktur,* which does not mean 'objectivity' but approximately the structure of the objects. In each case one must, then, discover the object's structuration in relation to the specific problematic, but without rejecting the old objects by considering them merely as false. One must always pose the question of the origin, the function, and the necessity of these false objects, which only become understandable in relation to the praxis and thought of a social group.

The example of Pascal's writings could also demonstrate the transformation of the object on the basis of changes in formulating the problem. For most Pascal scholars his works, the *Pensées* and the *Provinciales,* were the expression of the thought of Pascal the individual, who could not have changed his perspective in the time lapse which separated the publication of the two works. Their research dealt with the two texts as a single object. The *Provinciales* — written in collaboration with the Cartesians Arnauld and Nicole — were privileged by these researchers (for the most part Cartesians) because of their proximity to the Cartesian perspective. Now, it is impossible to establish a valid coherence for the two texts at one and the same time: each, in fact, possesses its own structuration and coherence. They are two different objects, and the problem of their genesis should be studied in relation to a collective subject, since, theoretically, the subject of a work or an action is never an isolated individual. In the research which led to *Le Dieu caché*, the problem was resolved rapidly enough with regard to the *Provinciales*. The solution was discovered in all the notebooks which discussed Arnauld and Nicole abundantly. For the *Pensées*, on the other hand, whose origin was confused with the *Provinciales*, nothing existed. Empirical research was necessary to discover the group of Barcos, the extremist Jansenist group opposed to Arnauld and Nicole and completely concealed by historians. It appeared then, that, when Pascal wrote the *Provinciales*, another Jansenist group criticized these writings, and that Pascal knew of this criticism. Thus, the rapid change of the Pascalian positions and the transition to the extremist tragic vision provoked by the condemnation of the Church became explicable.[2] At the start of the research, therefore, the current representation of the common consciousness was the departure point, the first state of the object studied. But it had to be transformed, restructured. In the process certain elements had to be abandoned, whereas other elements appeared. The *Provinciales* was no longer a part of the object when the structuration of the tragic world vision of the *Pensées* was elaborated, but on this level, the tragedies of Racine which are a part of it, were able to be integrated into this new object.

One cannot approach works or actions without beforehand raising the problem of their coherence, a coherence which can be made into a pattern, and then seeking the collective subject for which this coherent structure has a functional character, that is to say, constitutes for it an element of its possibility of existence. The structure is not only formal, as it is for contemporary structuralists who eliminate the function, the subject and development. Likewise, when we speak of the object's transformation, it is not a matter of the change in the object during the course of history, as positivism believes, nor of the progress in knowledge, but of transformations in the significant relation between the collective subject and the historical world, in other words, in the object's functionality. If, in effect, the object studied is a structure which only exists as a functional value for praxis, then it is impossible to understand the very nature of that object without the close bond with praxis. When one is dealing with theory, with thought, one must take into account the fact that differences of praxis — the praxis of classes and of various groups — require more or less elaborate, more or less adequate, theories and this relation between theory and practice which, according to Lukács, should attain its greatest transparence in the case of the proletariat, is always a mediated and functional relation.

If one grasps the fundamental and necessary character of this functionality, one can no longer admit the existence of general and permanent forms, such as art, painting, law, or ethics, general and abstract forms to which history repeatedly gives a different content. For each case it is important to question both the form and the necessity of its function which do not remain the same in the different cases, save in exceptional instances. Therefore, if we take law for an example, one must examine the form of the law in a specific society before undertaking any other research. For the forms of law are not identical, because their functions are different within different societies: it is even possible for a society structured in a different manner to lack this specific form. Also, the majority of the subjects taught in the universities do not exist: there is no history of law, of painting, or of literature. That would imply the belief that the history of literature, for example, is an object whose evolution, or 'becoming', is immanent and can be understood immanently. But, Mallarmé cannot be understood by starting from Ronsard, even if one considers all the literary mediations. In fact, the significant evolution is the evolution of the global society and not the evolution of some particular domain or other whose autonomy only rarely exists, and for very special sectors. It is true that painters define themselves in relation to each other and that writers discuss things among themselves. Yet, the basis of these relations — or the absence of them — between painters and poets through time, that which produces similarities and differences, that which makes possible or impossible relations, borrowings, oppositions and interpretations, the basis of all these positive and negative relations, is situated in global history and in the evolution of totality.

The particular case of the history of the sciences is rather different. First, because in the sciences the results are cumulative: former knowledge, that which is still accepted, is part of current theory and not of history. Since one is dealing here with a cumulative technique, history, for its part, has a particular value which historians of art and philosophy cannot lay claim to. Nevertheless, it is one of the claims to glory of the French school of scientific historians — of Koyré and Lenoble — to have introduced a basić revolution in the manner of compiling scientific history. According to these historians of the French school, only the chemical researcher — or some other man of science — can solely be interested in a history of science where only theoretical progress is reported and the earlier discoveries, which still form a real part of theory, are recalled. The history of science as a real historical object — Koyré and Lenoble said — must concern itself with errors and setbacks. Koyré and Lenoble situated themselves outside the Marxist and dialectical perspective, but rightly upheld the necessity of understanding each success among numerous failures, and of asking, for example, not who once discovered the law of gravity, but why all the others, those who were very near to this discovery and were not able to make it, why all these others baulked at the discovery Newton was to formulate. But these questions, and the research necessary to reply to them, no longer depends only on the immanent history of science, but also requires a history of mental categories. And to compile a history of such categories, one must orient oneself toward the history of global society. The autonomy of the sciences — a very relative autonomy, since a very short time ago we witnessed the interventions and uses of biology outside its own domain — depends upon the transformation of production and the changing of mental categories. Since the end of the nineteenth century, the value of all scientific progress has been admitted and recognized, but this autonomy is recent and entirely relative. Even in the case of the history of modern science, one cannot disregard the

history of global society, still less when it is a matter of
scientific history in the past.

History becomes important in a different way when it is a
matter of the history of philosophy or the history of theories
in the human sciences. Each of these categories came of the
development of totality, and is bound to the praxis of a
collective subject acting in the world. These relations
between theory, praxis, the collective subject and the world
are transformed and transform both the problem and the
manner of approaching and constituting it. Each past theory
is a significant object in relation to a group to be discovered
by research. It must be understood on the basis of the praxis
of that group, as having been elaborated in order to resolve a
certain number of problems. The latter have been transformed, just as the replies which had been given to them are,
with practical transformations.

Thus, the history of the problem, in the case of philosophy, the human sciences, and even (to a certain extent) the
natural sciences, is none other than the problem of history
itself. The history of the problem shows how subject-object
and functionality have changed in history with the praxis of
groups. As Lukács consistently recalls, an entire series of
classical Marxist works have always devoted one section to
the history of previous doctrines and their objects. Marx
intended to dedicate the fourth book of *Capital* to 'the
history of economic doctrines'; Rosa Luxemburg in *The
Accumulation of Capital* and Lenin in *The State and
Revolution* deal at length with the history of the problem of
accumulation or of the state. The historical sections of these
works do not in the least resemble the historical elements of
the problem which are usually found in the textbooks. If, for
example, these manuals are concerned about the theory of
trade, they present − in a preliminary chapter without
scientific interest, but following university conventions − the
various former or contemporary theories on trade and offer
accurate items of information which are left totally unrelated
one to the other, or, on the contrary, ingenuously seek to
establish an immanent evolution. Inversely, we have the
important aspect of the history of the problem, in that it
does not seek to establish an immanent and fictive evolution

at the theoretical level, at the level of the problem, but seeks to enable one to understand the history of the problem as the symptom of an immanent evolution in history at an incomparably more original level. In the great Marxist works which we have just cited, the history of theories is bound to the development of totality where those theories are born as functional realities for collective subjects who are in the world. It is thus, we believe, that a valid origin of the object can be found, where current theory, which must know its origin, has taken its place as a stage in the history of a totality which is evolving.

History and function are indissolubly bound to the subject and to meaning in its totality. This conception, which is basic according to Lukács and Marx, is far from being shared by all those who profess Marxism. The Althusser school, for example, which starts from very coherent mechanist positions, simultaneously rejects all of these categories and does not allow meaning any more than it allows function, the subject, history, or totality. Recently, the translator of Feuerbach's *The Essence of Christianity,* published by Althusser in the collection which he is editing, presented a great dilemma in his preface, entirely new so he believes, concerning philosophical thought, or rather contemporary theoretical thought. The translator illustrates this dilemma in his preface with two names, Spinoza or Feuerbach, and explains it in roughly the following words: one either postulates a meaning — which according to him is necessarily hidden, a kind of circular delirium of totality, like every dialectical interpretation of Marxism is, it appears — and then one finds oneself on the side of Feuerbach who remains an idealist because he seeks a meaning, even though purely human, in religion. Or, on the other hand, one no longer seeks meaning, but rather the method of production, which generates the immediate appearance of meaning, and in this case one finds oneself with Spinoza. Moreover, it is a matter of a much more mechanistic Spinoza than that of the real system. It is the Spinoza of the second kind of knowledge in the *Ethics,* cut off from the third kind which is just as essential, if not more so. In this dilemma something persists: whatever the interpretation one chooses, in fact, the immediate given remains the departure point toward the search for the method of production or the search for meaning.

This alternation between Spinoza and Feuerbach continues, in a new guise, a famous dichotomy, which has long dominated an entire section of Marxist literature as well as certain trends in academic science. 'Orthodox' Marxists were in the habit of calling upon a philosophy to answer the question and of defining themselves as materialist or idealist. This question could just as well be translated today by the new terms 'negation of meaning' or 'the search for meaning'. For Stalinists, it was useless to compile a history of philosophy (the question and its dilemma were broadly adequate) as though a label of materialism or idealism could render comprehensible, or explain, the meaning of a philosophy. This same alternation was also found outside Stalinism. It was translated by the opposition between comprehension and explanation in the methodology of the sciences of the spirit for German academicians and the phenomenologists. According to these academicians, the search for meaning should proceed, by means of a comprehensive attitude, with intuition and empathy. Otherwise, one was condemned to positivism, which studies the mode of production of a work causally, for example, according to the pattern of the natural sciences, and cannot at all understand the phenomenon studied. For Stalinists, to be scientific it was necessary to claim to be a materialist and, reciprocally, in claiming to be a materialist one became scientific. In a complementary way, according to the theorists of empathy, as soon as one sought for explanations, one deviated from science.

Nevertheless, since Hegel, at a scarcely scientific but methodologically formulated level, and subsequently since dialectical materialism and the writings of Marx, this alternative was to be completely rejected. Materialism and idealism — these are the two complementary faces of the same false attitude, which reduces material reality to the machine, and places meaning either in or outside the mind. In the first and the third of the *Theses on Feuerbach*, Marx expressed himself very clearly on this problem. According to him, Feuerbach eliminated activity in order to separate intuition and sensa-tion which ought to put us into relation with the object, but, as a result of this separation and this elimination, activity becomes the prerogative of idealism and theory. When reality and men are understood as machines, according to the old materialism, meaning is placed elsewhere, and one is forced to imagine, according to the third of the *Theses on Feuerbach,* some individuals — supermen or theorists — above society, who are the bearers of meaning and are able to act. But, the search for meaning is not exclusive of the search for the method of production, any more than the search for the method of production is from the search for meaning. Dialectics eliminates the dualist alternatives between materialism and idealism, determinism and voluntarism, be-tween the formalism of abstract historical periodizations and the irrationality of imperceptible individuals who burst in on history. Dialectics is, in its foundation and its beginnings, monist, and for it meaning is found in human reality and is transformed like it. Each structure possesses its own meaning which resides in its global signification, in its unity, and its structuration, which can only be understood in relation to the method of production, that is to say, by starting from the broader structuration which generates this meaning and in relation to which it constitutes a significant structure.

This relation between meaning and the method of produc-tion, between comprehension and explanation, is a problem of concrete and progressive totalities. One of Pascal's *Pensées* — to take an example from research already completed — must first be understood within the context of the *Pensées* as a whole, and the latter in their relation to all of Pascal's work, which in its turn must be explained on the basis of the broader totality constituted by the Jansenist movement. The work of Pascal has a comprehensive value in relation to Jansenism which, in turn, explains it. Jansenism itself permits us to understand the nobility of the cloth, while the nobility of the cloth explains the Jansenist movement. Further, the situation of the nobility of the cloth must be understood and explained in the context of class relations in seventeenth century France and to other world visions which they have generated, and so on. It is this whole procedure, both explanatory and comprehensive, which draws us closer and closer to the meaning of one of Pascal's thoughts and the method of its production which cannot be separated from it. It is always a matter of discovering the concrete mediations which transgress the alternatives of dualist thought because reality is not separate from meaning: it is both material and significant at the same time.

Research, which must deal with both meaning and the method of production, must also be able to fulfil four conditions in order to achieve valid results. If the object studied is a book, one must begin by seeking the world vision underlying it, as well as the group in relation to which this vision possesses a character of functional necessity, independently of course of the viewpoints of the researcher and his value judgments. Second, for a better elaboration of the world vision and the possible consciousness of the group, research must be oriented later on toward the global society. It must examine the adequacy of the group's world vision and its possible consciousness in relation to society as a whole in order to determine its ideological character or its truthfulness. The researcher studying a past epoch is standing outside it, at a certain historical distance, and he can better understand the whole of the relations between the different groups at that epoch which those living in, and creating at that epoch were unable to do at a conscious level. This distance abolishes in no way the identity of the subject and the object. It makes this identity relative each time and in a different manner. But it is necessary even for the present age — despite all the differences that presupposes and which must be overcome in order to achieve this distance — in order to constitute the significant structure of a work, or of an event, and in order to discover the mediations which explain its origin. The subject-object identity is situated at a level which is fundamental in a different way, in the original orientation toward the object, an orientation which itself comes from within the totality, of a moment of history just as the object of research is. Therefore, the ensemble of the world visions of groups, living and acting in a global society, must be constituted, and with regard to each of these groups, the researcher must examine the more or less ideological character of its world vision, that is to say, the maximum consciousness that each group was able to attain and which must not be confused with real psychological consciousness.

Nevertheless, this subjective consciousness and the subjective goals must also be studied, and the search for them constitutes the third element of the study. The level of subjective consciousnesses is often of secondary importance. That is why we have neglected it so far. But the subjective project, which is consciously subjective, can at times be very important and must not be systematically neglected. It is not only a matter of the immediate and subjective consciousness of those who are creative but also, and above all, of the real consciousness of groups who are the true subjects. After having connected the non-conscious rationality of the group's behaviour to its possible consciousness, which discloses its meaning, one must find out how this rationality is manifested in the real, subjective, consciousness of the group. And, finally, the fourth stage, which returns to the first two parameters of the research, must discover the social equilibrium toward which the action of the group tends, although this equilibrium, the result of the action of different groups, only very rarely corresponds — as we have already emphasized — to the subjectively conscious goals of the groups participating, or even to the non-conscious projects which govern their actions and which only the allocated consciousness can render explicit.

Meaning and the method of production, although inseparably bound, must be distinguished one from the other in the strategy of research. This begins with the search for meaning and must constitute the world vision before being able to undertake the other three complementary levels. This meaning is neither hidden nor esoteric. Though manifest, it is not immediately obvious because our mental structures are less and less apt immediately to accede to meaning and totality, because our social relations are extremely mediated. It very often occurs that even the global structuration, which constitutes the meaning and can only be grasped by its insertion in another broader structuration, is not immediately obvious and requires an entire series of mediations before it can be grasped. In the Middle Ages when theological meanings were asserted according to which God effectively intervened in reality, these global meanings also needed analysis, but they were almost immediately obvious and did not require the complement of a preliminary, fully analytical discussion. When the novel, corresponding to empiricism and rationalism without a global vision, became the literature of the partitioned world, in this world — which is also that of individualism — the individual was an immediately visible reality on the level of history and perception. The goal of these novelists was obviously the aggregate of the relations between the individual and the universe, but they already had to take a long detour to lead the reader to this global meaning, beyond anecdote. The detour became more and more prolonged between Don Quixote, still attached to certain values, and the life of Madame Bovary, which at first sight does not rise above the anecdotal level or that of the simple narration of events. The distance became wider and wider between the immediately perceived and the global meaning (which is, however, manifestly there); and for us, who no longer have an immediate perception of totality, the detours and mediations involve complications.

It is not, then, a matter of discovering an esoteric meaning which the researcher should introduce into the work from outside, but of re-establishing the unity to which one does not inevitably have immediate access. The process of comprehension demands construction and reflection, and the latter is both comprehensive and explanatory. The research must result in an analysis which is both rational and concrete. Only in this way can it go beyond the other interpretative attempts because it accounts for the whole without having to refer it to something abstract or general, such as laws. Because, while it comprehends the work as a work of art — but without transforming it into the unique and the imperceptible — it inserts it into historical evolution where it discovers its function. In each individual case one must research both the work's structure as a unit and the mediations in relation to the global society which enable this structure to be brought to light and its functionality shown. If these questions do not direct research, it remains trapped in the two attitudes we have already discussed: the purely formalist explanation and the type of comprehension which considers genius and the imperceptible.

But how is this manifest, yet at first sight hidden, meaning constituted? It is the aim of research to discover and constitute it but, of course, it does not bestow it arbitrarily from outside. Research brings out the meaning from the object which is also constructed in the very movement of research which brings out this meaning from it, an object which only completely exists with the appearance of the meaning which enables one to apprehend it as a significant structure. One does not approach a given object with universal pre-established rules, but with a functional conception of the object as a significant structure and with a methodological conception. It is a fact that even independently of their constitution in research, meaning and the object are already produced in the praxis of a plural subject. And research, which attempts to constitute this meaning and object, only ends up with results to the extent that it finds enough relations in the object to discover its necessary coherence, in other words its functionality for a collective subject. Outside of this relation of meaning and functionality, meaning must be able to account for the whole of phenomena under research in an immanent way, that is (to continue the example of the work of art), the aggregate of elements constituting a work and the links between them. Of the four stages which we have distinguished above in the strategy of research, it is the first which we have just defined, by insisting upon concrete and positive criteria which guarantee the validity of the procedure even before the other three stages are undertaken, dealing respectively with the adequation of the world vision to reality, with subjective finality, and with the objective result of any action and work.

Coherence should not be understood in a logical sense, in the belief that everything which does not immediately conform to logic, everything which implies a contradiction, is incoherent. Coherence must be conceived as relative, as functional, in relation to a social group and on the basis of its praxis. The tragic contradiction was a coherent world vision for the extremist Jansenists, and it was visible and necessary for them as a contradiction. But a world vision can just as well be contradictory and coherent, it can even have coherence within contradiction, without the latter appearing and being visible to the group from within. For example, in liberal ideology, the ideas of liberty and equality (taken in an absolute sense) are mutually exclusive. In fact, extreme liberty denies equality, and extreme equality denies liberty. Yet, they are found together in enlightenment thought, and they played a major role in the fight against feudalism. They were linked together and, despite everything that one can say about it now, they were not simply verbal assertions. It is necessary to study their function at each historical moment. Liberty and equality began to oppose one another to become, later on, manifestly contradictory, during the course of the nineteenth century, but they were not opposed to each other in the eyes of the progressive bourgeoisie. For this group, this present contradiction had coherence, although unformulated. Obviously – one now knows, and historical studies have demonstrated it very well – the bourgeoisie only wanted equality up to a certain point because this purely juridical equality was useful to them, but all the same, they wanted equality within those limits. Still, this new contradiction does not pose the problem of incoherence either, but rather that of ideology. It is a problem of false consciousness, of the difference between what the consciousness can aim for and what actual praxis wants to and can attain.

Coherence bound to function is constituted on the level of mental structures starting from the given historical situation and in the perspective of a specific praxis of a group in relation to other groups. Although generated by it as one of its essential elements, which sustain it and render it possible, ideology rarely corresponds to the praxis which it gives rise to, although it also is the result of this praxis. This correspondence or non-correspondence between ideology and praxis is the object of the second of the four stages of research which, at this level, poses the problem of the adequation of a world vision to reality and confronts ideology and praxis in order to comprehend their differences in the attempt to give an explanation for them.

In their action and for their existence, groups tend toward

coherence and in their praxis elaborate a functional coherence implicit in their mental structures, and in their daily, political, social, and economic behaviour. But this implicit significant coherence is rarely manifested in their consciousness. According to a famous work by Lukács on the guerilla soldier, it is the exception for a group to accept its world vision because groups are taken up completely in immediate tasks and the expression of such a world vision would very often involve immediate difficulties at the level of these tasks. The group never automatically produces the individual in order that he may express its world vision. To come back again to the example cited, the Pascalian philosophy of the just sinner, which the Church condemns, could not suit the Jansenists, although it may have expressed their world vision, because they were afraid of publicly producing texts which the Church could have condemned. Pascal, moreover, only wrote the *Pensées* when he had separated from Jansenism. Likewise, Racine wrote and had performed plays which structurally correspond to the tragic vision of Jansenism, but the latter, for its part, disapproved of theatrical activities in any form, whether it was the writing or the staging of plays.

One could just as well take an example from another area. Some years ago, as a sign of liberalization, the Soviets showed the films of Dziga Vertov at Florence during a festival dedicated to *cinéma-vérité*. Dziga Vertov had trouble with the Stalinist authorities and disappeared; we had always thought, according to what had been told us, that his work was the work of a rebel. But, if we see the films of Dziga Vertov who, we repeat, had serious trouble before disappearing, one now realizes that it is a question of a veritable epic of Stalinism and, therefore, unbearable for Stalinists. Vertov showed the difficulties and the poverty; for example, he filmed nurseries where children were scantily dressed and poorly nourished, whereas Stalinists wanted a marvellous and convincing picture of their indisputable success. It is an epic in the sense that Vertov shows all the difficulties facing the Stalinists and, according to his films, they acted with discipline and courage. Dziga Vertov in relation to the Stalinists, Pascal and Racine in relation to the Jansenist group, Jean Genet in relation to the radical French Left, distance themselves (and Jean Genet continues to do so) noticeably, a fact necessary for an understanding and explanation of their works.

In fact, a certain distance is necessary between the individual who expresses the world vision and the group which implicitly elaborates the possibility of this vision in its praxis. A certain liberty is necessary in order to lead this world vision to full coherence, as the great works do. But the genesis of the work and the world vision which the work is an expression of (in other words the genesis of the form, of the significant structure), is only intelligible in relation to the historical praxis of a collective subject and not in relation to the psychology or the existence of an individual subject or creator. It would be difficult to discover the purely psychological reasons which, in the space of a few months, were able to transform Pascal's perspective and cause him to produce works as different as the *Provinciales* and the *Pens*ées. In order to understand the genesis of these works, we must know the history of the relations between the Church and Jansenism, and above all, the existence of the heterogeneous groups within the Jansenist movement.

The collective subject under question here is not a renewed version of the Cartesian *ego,* which would replace the latter with a philosophical and abstract entity situated in, or rather facing the world. The group is not above the individuals who constitute it by their actions, in common or otherwise. It is individuals who act and are mutually corrected in the network of relations, which modify in this way what the others do, and constitute groups. The subject is trans-individual, plural or collective, and at the same time it is an object. The subject and the object are identical in the totality from whence they come: the group is born of the actions which it generates.

5 The Topicality of the Question of the Subject[1]

What we observe today in the industrially advanced countries of the West is the development of wealth as a condition of socialism, but also, because of the particular terms and conditions of this development, as its main obstacle. This wealth seems to seal off the horizon and hinder all creativity, without which socialism could not be achieved and would have no meaning. Creativity does not originate in the individual but comes from the actions of every member of society, and these actions are essential for cultural life and the creative acts of individuals. Evidently, society is not homogeneous. It is constituted of classes and groups which try to impose their views or combat the dominant viewpoints. But at the moment, the situation seems to be oriented more and more toward a dominant dogmatism of the *de facto* situation and a passive criticism which can say 'No' without having the possibility of changing anything.

Although the process of reification in liberal society has caused the disappearance of any community dimension from the consciousness of individuals, it has not, so far, abolished all activity. The individual could act, even if his activity necessarily led to failure, because the realization of the individual — the individualism promised by liberal society — is impossible. The great classical novels of the nineteenth century were based on this contradictory relation, whose theory was elaborated by Lukács. Nevertheless, even this form of activity has been rendered inaccessible, or it has been seriously impoverished, along with the works which correspond to it. Genetic structuralism has very quickly recognized the importance of Robbe-Grillet and Nathalie Sarraute. These are both great writers, yet the standards for them are not the same as for Stendhal, Balzac, or Flaubert, to cite only writers of this recent period during which the process of reification was already advanced. It is not a question of talent here, but of historical possibilities.

With the particular terms and conditions of the development of wealth in Western societies, the risk arises of dividing society into two groups, one of which — the strongest numerically — would be fundamentally condemned to passivity, and the other — the technocracy — would monopolize all decision-making.

The technocrats should be distinguished very clearly from the bureaucrats. Max Weber had analysed the structure and function of bureaucracy as a necessary element of liberal capitalism. It is a mechanism with precise and abstract rules which functions independently of any individual intervention which, on the contrary, is presented as a cause of disturbances. Technocracy is essentially different. Here we are concerned with a group which monopolizes the decision-making; a group capable, by its very decisions, of avoiding all bureaucratization, of adapting itself, of making effective decisions beyond abstract rules. Outside this group and its powers, the whole of society is fundamentally reduced to being a mere passive performer.

Since 1946 in the West, there have been only slight depressions because technocracy has succeeded in avoiding the great crises of overproduction. Currently, it is tending to raise the level of consumption higher and higher. With the considerable development of productivity, with the removal of crises and the assurance of material well-being, technocracy hopes to be able to confine the mass of society in a basic passivity. In fact, the absence of crises — of pauperization, as Marx thought — could hinder an awareness of the situation, since consumption renders passivity bearable. This consumption even monopolizes culture. The development of productivity requires competent executives and a high level of schooling. The massive production of automobiles is followed by the mass production of university diplomas, and illiterate university professors who, outside the area of their own speciality, may remain completely ignorant and passive. An enormous mass of information is delivered to people less and less capable of giving it form and understanding it. The diploma and the paper-back should not mask this false consumer culture. That is the danger menacing us and not the problems of productivity and development.

The mental structures are obstacles which one must conquer jointly with the economic and social difficulties. Every action which might separate the two would be condemned to failure, criticism would fall into the consumption which it denounces. Action and criticism can no longer be based on what ought to be, a moral postulate asserted by some as a norm. Criticism can only be developed as an objective possibility, as possible consciousness bound to the possibilities of action.

It is still necessary for thought to be able to orient itself toward the possible and toward action. This contradicts an entire section of contemporary thought. In fact, in this new situation, with organizational capitalism, a structuralist ideology has also developed which only managed to become dominant at the end of the Algerian war, even though some of its representatives had begun their work earlier. Structuralism was not developed from the viewpoint of the technocrats, but starting from this middle class, university educated or otherwise, which became more and more passive. It is essentially characterized by the negation of the subject and of activity, and implicitly, by the rejection of history and content which are bound to the first two concepts. Starting from this negation, two possibilities emerge: on the one hand, the study of formal, transhistorical structures following the linguistic model, as practised by Lévi-Strauss; on the other, one could cite Foucault who made very precise scientific analyses of existing structures and yet affirmed that meaning, if it exists, is only in madness and the unconscious, beyond any subject. For Althusser, a Marxist version of structuralism also exists which asserts the existence of structures within history, without any relation to human activity. These are entities which act; they are there, but science is incapable of knowing where they come from or how they are transformed. Science is incapable — or will only be capable in the distant future — of explaining how one passes from one structure to another. By eliminating human activity, structuralism has rendered the problem of this passage insoluble.

For years, *genetic structuralism* found itself in opposition to existentialism, which defined the individual and the concept of liberty in an abstract way. We have defended structures against this subjectivization of everything possible by showing that limitations are not only external but also constitute man's psychic structure, by insisting on the transindividual character of subjects. Now that the crisis period of capitalism has passed, with the setting up of self-regulatory mechanisms, structuralism rejects the basic philosophical problems. For Althusser it is no longer a question of man, and even this false concept — ideological, according to him — is meaningless and without any theoretical function in the social sciences. It is the relations of production which create historical situations and impose roles on men. Of course, this is one aspect of the Marxist conception and it is fundamental; but it should not cause the other aspect to be forgotten according to which the relations of production are nothing but relations between men, relations produced on the basis of previous historical situations.

This new Althusserian interpretation of Marxism, its influence and success, must be understood in this new economic and ideological context. When this transformation was effected and structuralism began to develop, eventually assuming a dominant position, a great many young thinkers, intellectuals and students found themselves in a difficult and painful situation. They were sympathetic toward Marxism, or rather had been trained in it. Already thrown in confusion by destalinization, moreover, they were carried along in the new structuralist trend. Their situation was difficult and conflicting. A book such as Lucien Sebag's *Marxisme et structuralisme,* which presented problems first in the Marxist perspective and then from the structuralist angle, finally opting for structuralism, expressed this agonizing situation well. Lucien Sebag committed suicide, which for the new generation of thinkers was a major loss because Sebag was one of its most promising members. But the problematic of Sebag was not peculiar to him, it was that of a whole group of young thinkers until the arrival of Althusser. Louis Althusser demonstrated that conflict does not exist; he has dispersed the differences between Marxism and structuralism, even if, to do so, he has had to break down Marx's texts to discover their combinative elements, assembly, mechanism, etc. Althusser especially criticized Marx's humanism by presenting Marxism as a profoundly antihumanist thought, and he criticized a concept — which is used for every purpose: that of alienation. It is difficult to admit the elimination of man in the interpretation of Marx, since man is under discussion in nearly all of the *Theses on Feuerbach.* But man is not an individual subject as is apparently believed by the structuralists, and Althusser, who reject him. Man is not the origin of the structure. This very problem of knowing which came first, man or the structure, is a false problem which has no place in dialectics. The fact remains, however, that the Althusserian criticism of the concept of alienation is partly valid. Alienation is too vast to be able to constitute an operative scientific concept, whereas reification is more precise. But a new concept of alienation must be elaborated in order to be able to account for the present reality, just as the entire aspect of Marxist theory with regard to the revolutionary proletariat (which does not correspond to historical reality) should be revised.

The development of organizational capitalism has not only permitted the development of structuralism. It has also involved alterations in the thought of those who had a critical attitude: in Lukács — even independently of former repudiations — and in the thought of those who appealed to the young Lukács.

Even today (1968), Lukács conceives of work and action as starting from global history but, contrary to former practice, he no longer connects its origin to the praxis of groups and, for the present day major work, to the most advanced group of society which tends to go beyond the present structures. Important work or thought, according to the Lukács of today, is important through the relation of the individual, who produces them, to global history. It is this individual relation to history, one which is no longer revealed and constituted in the praxis of a privileged group, which sustains the creation and offers a basis for its validity.

Adorno and the members of the Frankfurt School sided with the young Lukács and published many of his articles — matchless at that time — in the review of their institute. They themselves wrote remarkable books of dialectical analyses, but now they have changed and maintain different and even opposite conceptions.

Adorno revealed his new conceptions at a recent congress on the sociology of literature, as, moreover, had Agnes Heller (one of Lukács's closest collaborators) on behalf of Lukács. According to Adorno, the creator situates himself outside reality, not at this necessary distance from the group whose world vision he expresses, but outside of reality, and his attitude toward it is extremely critical: a minimal acceptance and a maximal rejection. That leads Adorno to the idea of a purely negative dialectic, to rejection, and to the requirement of the impoverishment of content, an impoverishment and rejection for which the ideal would be Beckett. In almost Heideggerian tones — whom he criticizes sharply, moreover — Adorno now rejects everything which is popular, and any concession to the popular, and thus arrives, through criticism, at rather conservative positions.

He conceives of the work as a sort of objective reality, a nearly Platonic reality or form which the creator should attain. To defend the idea of this constraint by form, Adorno recalls that, however great a genius he may be, the creator could only produce everything he wants to at the risk of succumbing to mediocrity. This is incontestable at the psychological level of the individual, but in no way does it explain to us the existence of its objective realities, nor their origin. As we have seen, this objective reality — in other words coherence, significant structure, aesthetic form, which goes beyond the subjective consciousness of the individual creator — is not in the least a Platonic reality, but rather the possible consciousness of a plural object, its world vision. This objectivity, this form, exists for the individual who must attain it not as an evident reality, but as a non-conscious norm; it is here that the individual is differentiated from the collective subject, because, in the historical praxis of a plural subject, the forms are neither given nor are they pre-existent. It is by starting from this collective praxis that the forms become intelligible and that their genesis can be grasped.

Moreover, Adorno is little interested in these significant structures. What makes a work important for him, what interests him, is what he calls its 'truth content'. This truth content, according to his pronouncements on it at the congress, is difficult to define and always goes beyond the purely intellectual. Consequently, the work must not be approached in its totality and by following its genesis, but in relation to criticism, to the philosopher, who knows this truth content today. Literature no longer appears interesting or valid except to the extent that the critical philosopher speaks about it in order to extract certain elements from it which he judges in relation to something which is not the work itself. Thus, the truth content is beyond the work, in the consciousness of the critical philosopher who chooses this content in accordance with the critical consciousness, and the work is no longer considered except outside itself. This truth content, then, is situated outside history or in the history of philosophy. As a result, aesthetics is subordinated to philosophy, to truth, to the theoretically valid content. And, since this truth content is not a significant structure inherent to the work, it becomes a sort of evidence, of which the cultured man, the thinker, the philosopher may have a sort of intuitive knowledge. Their knowledge is shared by other cultured men, without the existence of any foundation other than culture for this community. With much finesse and subtlety Adorno comes back to this Neo-Kantian thought and to the dualism of the subject and the object which Lukács and Heidegger had transcended, thus taking up the position of Bruno Bauer's and Max Stirner's *Critical Consciousness.*

This *Critical Consciousness* found an explanation in the young Marx and the young Lukács, on the basis of its historical genesis, and this can also clarify Adorno's new position. Following Marx's directions, Lukács was the first to overturn the old customary scheme of the development of Neo-Hegelian philosophy. He discusses the Neo-Hegelians in

History and Class Consciousness and in articles on Lassalle and Moses Hess of the same period. These ideas of Lukács, continued by A. Cornu in his books on M. Hess and Marx, are now very widespread and — as in the case of other Lukácsian ideas — their origin has been forgotten. The earlier history of Neo-Hegelianism was different. It constituted a chain which went from Hegel to the Neo-Hegelians, to those of the right, the centre, and the left, to reach Marx, as the most radical among the Hegelians of the left, who developed dialectical materialism. But Lukács has shown that those who are called 'Hegelians of the Left' are in fact closer to Fichte — as the Neo-Kantians were later on — than to Hegel. They had moved away from the Hegelian position, according to Lukács, because they had abandoned the fundamental categories of totality and the identity of the subject and the object, in order to return to the subject-object opposition in the form of the opposition between 'critical consciousness' and the world.

In *The Holy Family* and *The German Ideology* Marx had already accused the Hegelians of the left — Feuerbach, Bauer, Stirner, etc., — of having retained Hegel's language and his categories, but also for having returned to this side of Hegel, who tried to imagine himself in the world. In fact, the Hegelians of the left thought they were situated above the world and spoke from outside it, whereas according to Marx — and he ardently insists upon it in *The German Ideology* — when someone speaks, he should ask who is speaking and from where. The Hegelians of the left are in opposition to the reality of ideas which have no real basis: Bauer with his critical self-consciousness and Stirner with his egoistic individual which, Marx has shown, is not real and, in short, comes from a philosophical construction, just like Bauer's 'critical consciousness'. To know what one is speaking about, Marx very justifiably requires that one know who is speaking and from where: it is necessary to know that one always speaks from within a world from which comes the structure of consciousness of the one who is speaking and who, in order to know what he is saying, must know this world and this structuration at the risk of otherwise remaining within an ideology.

Marx was debating with the Hegelians of the left, his old friends and contemporaries, on the theoretical level with a view to the truth. Lukács proposes to us a genetic explanation concerning the appearance of this Neo-Hegelian 'critical consciousness', and to do so, he goes back to his source, Hegel. The latter, as a dialectical thinker, had to understand his own philosophy — to the extent that he was speaking from inside the totality and knew that he was doing so — as an awareness of the totality within, and starting from, the world, an idea we have rediscovered in Lukács and Heidegger. Hegel connected himself to a mundane historical reality to conceive of himself — that is to say, his philosophy — as a historical fact decisive in and for history. He did this by linking himself first of all with the French Revolution and Napoleon, as did Goethe, his contemporary, a dialectical writer who knew him and found himself faced with the same problems. But while Goethe, less prone than Hegel to theoretical compromises, subsequently sought an outlet by looking to America, Hegel turned toward the Prussian State and bureaucracy which, after the fall of Napoleon and when he was writing his *Philosophy of Right*, represented the most progressive elements of the period.

According to Lukács, the Hegelians of the left are the expression of a small radical group oriented since the beginning of the 1840s toward the revolution of 1848, without being sufficiently strong to succeed in the revolution, or capable of thinking about itself and the situation clearly. Moreover, after the failure of the revolution of 1848, the group altered and its thinkers (who had been very well-known) lost all importance. Beforehand, in the struggle against the Prussion State, which created all sorts of difficulties for them, the Hegelians of the left could not continue Hegel's compromise, nor find in Germany a real force which they could have relied on. And so they criticized the world as bad and negative without knowing where, in what place, and in what perspective or praxis, to situate their criticism. They placed it in an imaginary entity, a 'critical consciousness', or in the egoistic individual, Stirner's 'Unique Man' — who is another version of this — who opposes the world and judges it.

In *History and Class Consciousness,* where Lukács offers this explanation concerning the Hegelianism of the left, there is another important observation — likewise derived from Marx — on Hegel's philosophical limits and his proximity to Kant and Fichte. It is these limits of Hegel which have permitted the Hegelians of the left, and the Neo-Hegelians in general, to use him as their authority and to continue to use his language in order to uphold a Fichtean outlook. Lukács recalls that Hegel rejects any possibility of judgment coming from the outside because he develops a philosophy of immanence and totality. Yet, according to the Hegelian conception, history is the work of the Absolute Spirit which, although intervening through its agents, remains outside reality and has a dualist relationship with it. Thus, despite the monism of a system which denies dualism, a dualism of the subject and the object virtually exists in Hegel between the Absolute Spirit and concrete history, according to Lukács. This opposition of the subject and the object was able to be accentuated and placed at the centre of their preoccupations by the Hegelians of the left, for whom the Absolute Spirit simply became the subjective consciousness of the critique, the 'subject' of history.

According to Lukács, it is not because the young Marx had been the most radical of the Hegelians of the left, i.e. in reality a Fichtean, that he developed dialectical materialism. Quite the contrary, it was because he was the only consistent Hegelian among them that he eliminated all of the Fichtean and Kantian residues from the thought of Hegel and that he turned toward rigorously monist thought. And he only attained this thought, and was only able to elaborate it completely, after his exile in France and his discovery of the proletariat as the new social force and as the basis of identical theory and praxis.

Since Marx's time, and even since *History and Class Consciousness,* the development of the forces of production and economic relations has again rendered problematic the relation between thought and reality. Even Lukács abandoned the identity of the subject of praxis and the subject of the work, and no longer relates the work to the group, but to the relation of its creator to global history. Thus, the old theory of the revolutionary proletariat as the historical basis, by its action, of dialectical thought must be modified and can no longer be maintained or asserted as before. The Frankfurt School, which no longer admits this old conception, has the impression that the ground has been pulled away from under its feet. But this disappearance of the collective subject has not led it to join the structuralists who, on the basis of the technocratic structures of organizational capitalism, deny the existence of the subject. The Frankfurt School has kept its critical positions; nevertheless, it finds itself in the situation of the Hegelians of the left in the Germany of the 1840s. It has come back to the dualism between the subject and the object, and criticizes the world on the basis of ideas which it is far from being able to justify. Bauer came from Hegel. Today, Adorno comes from an earlier Adorno, close to the positions of *History and Class Consciousness,* who would not easily have accepted this radical rejection and this 'critical consciousness' which he upholds today, while continuing, on other points, his refined and intelligent dialectical analyses. The need to know worldly reality, the collective subject on the basis of which one thinks, obviously only exists for the dialectical thinker. Descartes — to take the famous example of a non-dialectical thinker — does not have such a problem and almost ignores its possibilities. The relation between the dialectical thinker and the worldly reality from which he begins, is a dialectical, circular, relation. The collective subject produces the mental structures which the thinker expresses and elaborates, and he must be able to account for their real origin in his thought.

If one does not accept Adorno's 'critical consciousness', which judges and scans reality from on high, or the individual relation to global history as Lukács currently conceives it, if one wishes to maintain, no longer the idea of the revolutionary proletariat, but the requirements of Marx's dialectical thought (which always demands that one know who is speaking and from where), of the subject-object totality, then the basic question arises of knowing who is, now, the subject of speech and action. It is necessary to know in the name of what and from where we are speaking today, if we believe that there are only valid works and actions to the extent that they are placed within a universe created by men and are attached to specific groups.

There are situations in which one cannot give an answer because the group, from which speech and action comes, is not yet manifest. In these situations, on the basis of a modified tradition, individuals speak by formulating perspectives and positions for which the group, the true subject, if it is not yet there, is in gestation or waiting to be elaborated. And very probably, these positions will be modified when the group becomes manifest.

Part 3

Being and Dialectics

Being and Dialectics[1]

One can neither think about Being nor act upon it in an adequate way, since it also embraces the subject of thought and action. Nor can one know Being adequately through intuition, since it also embraces the external world as it emerges in theoretical thought and action. The only way to gain access to the most valid bond between thought and action, on the one hand, and Being, on the other, is constituted by the attitude of a conscious wager of its status and ontological bases.

I

In an *immediate* way all reflection of consciousness upon itself and its status first of all affirms the separation of the subject and the object, the self and the world.

I think about a world which, as an object of my thought, has another epistemological status than my own consciousness. Likewise, I act upon a world which, as the object of my action, has a practical status different from myself, being one of the poles of a global structure of which I am the complementary pole.

Yet, as soon as reflection advances even a little, one perceives that it is difficult to accept this duality as such. Already pre-dialectical discussions between rationalism and idealism, before any reflection upon development, have shown us the existence of two opposed, complementary, and on the static level, equally founded positions; one which, by reducing the object to the subject, made the external world a simple modification of consciousness, and the other which, by reducing the subject to the object, makes consciousness a simple intramundane object analogous to all those considered by reflection.

Actually, however, the problem is complex in a different way, because for dialectical thought, the subject-object dualism proves to be both *real and relative*, being the principal manifestation of a fundamental unity which, to use two terms by which it has often been designated in contemporary philosophy, we can readily call: Being (Heidegger) or Totality (Lukács).

In fact, dialectical thought cannot radically separate the subject and the object, since all reflection about the external world discovers the latter as being by nature such that one day during its evolution it made possible and perhaps necessary, the appearance of life and consequently that of consciousness which at present conceives it.

Thus, from the beginning the object virtually harbours and makes possible that which at a moment of its genesis will become the subject of thought and action. Inversely, the subject is not content to understand nature and society, in taking cognizance of their structure. Its knowledge always proves to be narrowly bound to action, to the work which transforms them, so that the object, as object, and without in the least being reduced to a simple fact of consciousness is, nevertheless, largely the product of the subject whose structure and aspirations it expresses.

Without, then, falling into the unilateralism of idealism, which reduces the object to the subject, or into mechanistic materialism, which reduces the subject to the status of the object, we must establish that the subject-object dualism can only be validly conceived against a background of a more complex relation which recognizes in the subject, as subject, an objective nature and in the object, as object (partially the product of thought and men's labour), a subjective nature.

This means that the subject and object can only be validly conceived to the extent one succeeds in integrating them into a structured whole, Being or Totality, nevertheless characterized — and it is in this which the difficulty in formulating any dialectical thought exists — *by the fact that it cannot be*

either the object of adequate thought or the object of action.
This is so for the simple reason that all thought and action is
situated within *Being* and cannot go outside it to deal with it
as an object.

That is why, without falling into irrationalism and while
being entirely convinced that human reason will succeed in
elucidating more and more the nature of the cosmic and
human world, it seems to us that this elucidation can never
become complete and that an element of incertitude will
always remain in men's thought and action, bound to their
ontological status.

In addition to its explicative and moral functions, long ago
brought to light by sociologists, the idea of divinity was
perhaps *also* the expression of this unrealizable ideal of an
objective knowledge of Being, a contradictory ideal which
man cannot dispense with and which, nevertheless, he can
never effectively attain.

II

In this sense we readily agree with such thinkers as Lukács
and Heidegger when they assert that no thought, whether
indicative and imperative, theoretical and normative, can
grasp either Being in its entirety, or its nature in any partial
manifestation.

In effect, it is important to start from the basic distinction
between what Heidegger calls Being and Existence and
Lukács Totality (which includes the subject and the object)
and all objective knowledge or affirmation of value claiming
objectivity.

This distinction, moreover, is extended further than what
we have just said about it explicitly because not only is Being
or Totality situated at the level of the unity of the subject
and the object, whereas theory and norm are situated at the
level of their separation, but furthermore this separation of
the unitary structure of Being involves, actually within the
subject and object, relative and secondary separations —
without doubt inevitable for acting and living — but having a
more pragmatic than ontological validity. The most important among them is precisely that, both derived and

indispensable, between thought and action, theory and norm.

It seems very likely that in the beginning for all pre-human subjects, as well as for the infant, this distinction did not exist. The external world for them is *inseparably* both an object of knowledge and action. It should also be added that these terms constitute an anachronism to the extent that they introduce into the animal or infant universe concepts pertaining to the adult man, who asserts the original unity of entities for him definitively and irremediably separate.

The appearance of the dualism between theory and praxis, moreover, has had highly beneficial results for man, since it has made possible the division of labour, co-operation, and, with these, social life (which has, in turn, most likely been developed and strengthened by the latter).

The least act of co-operation going beyond instinctive reactions presumes, in effect, the separation (naturally relative and not radical) between theory and praxis. Already, for two men simply to lift a rock, it is necessary that one of the partners can designate the other, *at the theoretical level,* a share of the object: the rock, his own actions, what the other must do, the conditions of their co-ordination, and so on. At this price action upon nature becomes without doubt incomparably more powerful and efficacious than was that of the isolated individual. It nevertheless hides from immediate consciousness the relations between thought and action, and, for that very reason, the status of the subject within the totality, presenting to him as distinct and complementary elements what, across a varying number of mediations, in reality constitutes a fundamental unity.

Thus, with regard to the problem of the relations between thought and action, the same difference is repeated between the epistemological and practical levels, on the one hand and, on the other, the ontological level which we revealed for the subject-object dualism at the beginning of this essay.

III

There is, nevertheless, a problem which we wish to insist upon further: that which concerns the relations between these two levels and the difference, on this point, which separates the philosophical positions of Lukács from those of Heidegger.

For the latter the ontological and the ontic are two different spheres and, in the concrete unfolding of his analyses, entirely separate. The ontic pertains to the competence of science and morals,[2] and Heidegger seems fully to acknowledge the validity of scientific and even scientistic procedures for the purpose of his own comprehension.

Science has its own sphere within which it is both justified and self-sufficient. Philosophy, which refers to 'Being' and can only reach it via purely theoretical thought, is situated elsewhere, at a different level which seems to have nothing in common with the first. At the very most one could ask if for Heidegger these exceptional and special people, the philosophers, poets and statesmen, can themselves be the object of valid scientific (psychological and sociological) study.[3]

Lukács, on the contrary, and Marxist thinkers in general reject any distinction between science and philosophy.[4]

For them there is only one kind of valid knowledge: the attempt to reach the maximum adequation of thought to reality. It follows, nevertheless, that if in its totality this reality signifies the unity of the subject and object, it can only be validly grasped outside any philosophy at the theoretical or normative levels of their radical separation. That is why for the Marxist the problem of Being, the philosophical problem, is posed within, and *only* within, positive research.

And since all human thought, by nature, has a theoretical character, and since it cannot, for that very reason, grasp the totality, the problem of a positive understanding of reality becomes that of a *progressive* correction of the data of experience and reflection in their insertion into Being, so as to diminish ontologically inevitable distortions.

These corrections are carried out by a process of reflection which, however, remains conscious of the fact that it can never attain adequation to reality and which, without falling into relativism (since it admits the existence of a real progress of knowledge), cannot for that reason ever hope for an absolutely certain science or an action free from risk.

IV

The inadequation between theory and reality is an old philosophical subject, from Zeno of Elea's paradoxes to Pascal, who could only define man as he who 'infinitely surpasses man', which is both a paradox and, from the logical viewpoint, a contradiction.

If we reject the word 'infinitely', however, which implies transcendence, this definition seems to us the only one able to account for the simple empirical fact of progress, which presumes a development oriented in a positive direction (even if one reduces it to the domain where it is incontestable, that of the increasing mastery over nature).

Moreover, the concept of progress poses problems in turn and presents analogous antinomies. For even abstracting from the principal fact that all progress, in the sense of an increasing mastery over nature, is bound to an ensemble of social transformations and modifications of consciousness which present a less univocal aspect, because it would be difficult to say that national socialist society was certainly progressive in relation to the Greek city-state or that the best contemporary works of literature are at a higher level than the poems of Homer or Shakespeare's plays, it emerges that, even at the strictly technical level, the concept of progress is complex and ambivalent.

We can mention, for example, the fact that for a long period in the history of capitalism (today probably over with, although this is not absolutely certain), a certain rhythm of technical progress periodically ended in crises of over-production which, at times, arrested for a rather long while the development of the forces of production.[5] Likewise, the discovery of atomic fission created the risk of an immense destruction of the means of production and large-scale technical regression.

Finally, a current phenomenon of economic life, that of the lag of a social group in this or that technical sector is due precisely to the fact that it had already been in this same domain at the point of progress, and that it must absorb the old means of production at the economic level.

At the end of the nineteenth century, the superiority of

German industry was in the first place due to the late development of German capitalism which permitted it to be equipped with modern machinery at a moment when the other major capitalist countries (notably England and France) still had an immense technical apparatus to absorb. On a more modest level, the superiority of the French road system from 1930 to 1935 appears to us to be one of the principal reasons for the feeble development of motorways in France today.

When it is a question of the human sciences, one can see to what point every idea becomes complex, ambivalent, and full of risks of distortion, when one abstractly applies it to the comprehension of reality. Furthermore — Marx made this quite clear — it is not only the immediate application of general concepts which is abstract, but just as much so immediate empirical data.

A black is a black. It is only in certain social conditions that he becomes a slave, a tribal chief or, one should add today, a minister of an independent state. A machine is a machine. It is only in certain social conditions that it becomes capital and, therefore, a means of human exploitation or, on the contrary, the collective property of the community and thus a means of liberation.

One sees how, and to what extent, theoretical consciousness, from its most elementary to the highest levels, implies a simplifying distortion of reality, a distortion which it can progressively correct, according to its possibilities, by inserting the facts studied into broader and broader *relative totalities;* granted, however, that one remembers that these relative totalities are in a process of perpetual evolution, that this evolution is first of all the result of the action of men, and that this action is in turn found in close connection with their theoretical thought.

That is why, whatever the bias may be with which man approaches his status, his relation with the world, he finds himself, since he necessarily does so at the level of consciousness, involved in a circle which he can certainly enlarge, but from which he can in no way entirely escape.

We mention three particularly important examples to illustrate this situation:

(a) The problem of the classification of the sciences and its relation with the ontological structure of reality: everyone knows the linear classifications of the sciences which regard mathematics and logic as the most general sciences upon which are progressively founded the more and more specialized sciences such as physics, biology, and finally, such human sciences as psychology and sociology.

Only, one discovers that it is precisely the psychological and sociological reality which forms the basis for the validity of mathematics and logic which only exist in so far as psychic facts, the causal and genetic explanation of which precisely brings into relief the human sciences which linear classification situated at the opposite pole.[6]

(b) Similar difficulties arise when one broaches the frequently discussed problem of the causal relation between social circumstances and the behaviour of men. It is, in effect, true that the behaviour of individuals making up a group is to a very large extent determined by the whole of the economic and social circumstances to which it is attached and that the whole of these circumstances is nothing but the result of the behaviour of the individuals making up the group.

(c) Finally, to end this study, we will deal with the most important ontological problem: that of the relation between facts (theoretically established, the 'existents') and values. Again, as we have already said, this way of presenting the problem is anachronistic since it implies the separation of facts and values in its terminology.

In fact, for rationalist thought the latter constitutes an obvious axiom. Poincaré once formulated it in a classic way by saying that 'from two premises in the indicative, one can never draw a conclusion in the imperative'.

On looking more closely, we nevertheless observe that every fact which is known and thought is implicitly structured by an aggregate of values the nature of which is essentially social and which constitute the consciousness of the individual, whereas, on the other hand, all values, even when presented to this consciousness with the claim to the most absolute and universal validity, remain strictly bound to a certain social and economic structure which has its precisely determined historical place (although it may be difficult to know it) within human history, always open and in the process of being made (is there anything more historically determinate and localized than Kantian ethics?).

Hence all values are essentially grounded in facts which in their turn are intimately structured by values.

That means that once more we find ourselves confronting a distinction which is both indispensable and derivative, which could only be exceeded if, as much as possible, the object of every concrete analysis is inserted within ever larger relative totalities, totalities in relation to which the thinker must never forget that he finds himself within this broader totality, without doubt hierarchically structured, but unknowable at the theoretical level which we have called in this study Being and Totality.

It follows that despite the most penetrating and honest efforts to increase to the maximum the adequation of knowledge to its object and to the efficacy of action, neither could ever give man either absolute certitude or certain efficacity. That is why all positive reflection on the relationship between man and Being, or even more simply, between man and History, necessarily ends up in such ontologically fundamental concepts as: the effort to humanize reality — the necessity of incarnation, the hope of succeeding in this effort, the risk of failure, and — the synthesis of the three — the gambling element which is found at the centre of all thought which is truly and rigorously dialectical.

Notes

Part 1 Introduction to Lukács and Heidegger

1 See chapter 1 of Part 2.
2 G. Lukács, *History and Class Consciousness*, Massachusetts, MIT Press, 1968, pp. xlvi–xlvii.
3 *Ibid.*, p. 1.
4 *Ibid.*, p. 2.
5 *Ibid.*
6 *Ibid.*, p. 3.
7 *Ibid.*
8 *Ibid.*, pp. 3–4.
9 *Ibid.*, p. 5.
10 *Ibid.*, pp. 6–8.
11 *Ibid.*, pp. 8–9.
12 *Ibid.*, pp. 9–10.
13 *Ibid.*

Part 2 Lectures during the 1967–8 Academic Year

1 Reification, *Zuhandenheit* and Praxis
  1 This article is chapter 1 of Goldmann's posthumously published book *Lukács et Heidegger* (Paris: Denoël/Gonthier, 1973), pp. 91–105.

2 Totality, Being and History
  1 This article is chapter 2 of Goldmann's *Lukács et Heidegger* (Paris: Denoël/Gonthier, 1973), pp. 106–20.
  2 *Kierkegaard vivant* (Paris: Gallimard, Collection Idées, 1966) contains Lucien Goldmann's contribution to the colloquium organized by UNESCO on the occasion of the 150th

110

anniversary of Kierkegaard's birth. The essential passages of Lukács's essay on Kierkegaard are translated and commented on by Goldmann.

3 The passages from 'The Metaphysics of Tragedy' are reproduced here, in order to be more faithful to the original, from an old translation by Lucian Goldmann published in *Recherches dialectiques* (Paris: Gallimard, Collection Idées, 1959), pp. 251—3.

3 Objective Possibility and Possible Consciousness

1 This article is chapter 3 of Goldmann's *Lukács et Heidegger* (Paris: Denoël/Gonthier, 1973), pp. 121—39.

4 Subject-object and Function

1 This article is chapter 4 of Goldmann's *Lukács et Heidegger* (Paris: Denoël/Gonthier, 1973), pp. 140—62.

2 Cf. *Le Dieu caché* — study of the tragic vision in Pascal's *Pensées* and in Racine's plays (Paris: Gallimard, 1955).

5 The Topicality of the Question of the Subject

1 This article is chapter 5 of Goldmann's *Lukács et Heidegger* (Paris: Denoël/Gonthier, 1973), pp. 163—76.

Part III Being and Dialectics

1 Translated from L. Goldmann, 'Etre et dialectique', *Les Etudes philosophiques*, no.2, April—June, 1960, pp. 205—12.

2 To the restriction of metaphysics also. One also has the impression that Heidegger does not recognize the validity of metaphysics and that the latter is a hybrid for him, an attempt by philosophical thought which would have aimed for the onto-logical while entirely remaining, due to its purely theoretical procedures, at a level permitting it to grasp only the ontic.

3 To our knowledge, Heidegger never explicitly poses the problem, but it seems to us that his entire philosophy indicates a negative answer. No psychologist or sociologist, but only a philosopher could validly understand — and repeat in assuming them — the pre-Socratics, Hölderlin, or the politician who creates a state.

4 In order to be precise, one must also distinguish two currents in Marxist thought, one which identifies philosophy with science in general, the other only with the genetic sciences, and in particular, the human sciences. This is the famous discussion on the 'dialectics of nature', an inaccurate definition in our opinion because it would be better to designate it a

discussion on the dialectical character of the physico-chemical sciences. Lukács himself began by denying this character, only to assert it later on.

5 It is also true that very often the competition developed during a crisis was an active factor of technical progress.

6 See Jean Piaget, *Épistémologie génétique,* 3 vols (Paris: P.U.F.).